C000184949

Unsecured ladders

Unsecured ladders

Meeting the challenge of the unexpected

Graham Robinson

*Visiting Research Fellow, Centre for Management
Learning and Development, University of Surrey*

and

John Harris

formerly Chief Executive, Calor Group plc

© Graham Robinson & John Harris 2009

All rights reserved. No reproduction, copy or transmission of this publication may be made without written permission.

No portion of this publication may be reproduced, copied or transmitted save with written permission or in accordance with the provisions of the Copyright, Designs and Patents Act 1988, or under the terms of any licence permitting limited copying issued by the Copyright Licensing Agency, Saffron House, 6-10 Kirby Street, London EC1N 8TS.

Any person who does any unauthorized act in relation to this publication may be liable to criminal prosecution and civil claims for damages.

The authors have asserted their rights to be identified as the authors of this work in accordance with the Copyright, Designs and Patents Act 1988.

First published 2009 by
PALGRAVE MACMILLAN

Palgrave Macmillan in the UK is an imprint of Macmillan Publishers Limited, registered in England, company number 785998, of Houndmills, Basingstoke, Hampshire RG21 6XS.

Palgrave Macmillan in the US is a division of St Martin's Press LLC, 175 Fifth Avenue, New York, NY 10010.

Palgrave Macmillan is the global academic imprint of the above companies and has companies and representatives throughout the world.

Palgrave® and Macmillan® are registered trademarks in the United States, the United Kingdom, Europe and other countries

ISBN-13: 978-0-230-22230-4

This book is printed on paper suitable for recycling and made from fully managed and sustained forest sources. Logging, pulping and manufacturing processes are expected to conform to the environmental regulations of the country of origin.

A catalogue record for this book is available from the British Library.

A catalog record for this book is available from the Library of Congress.

10   9   8   7   6   5   4   3   2   1
18   17   16   15   14   13   12   11   10   09

Printed and bound in Great Britain by CPI Antony Rowe, Chippenham and Eastbourne.

To Katie, Daniel, Alfie and Siân who will face
the challenges that we shall leave behind.

Graham Robinson

To my wife Frances without whom there would be
nothing, and to our daughters Louise and Catherine
for being simply the best.

John Harris

CONTENTS

Dedications   v
List of boxes   x
List of figures   xi
Acknowledgments   xiii

Chapter 1   Introductions and a problem   **1**

1.1   What's the big idea?   1
1.2   Who we are   4
1.3   For whom are we writing this book?   4
1.4   Four areas of leadership choice and challenge   7
1.5   A major issue: why would you want to be a leader?   10
1.6   More challenges   13
1.7   Obligations and key messages   15
1.8   How to use the book   18
1.9   If you read this book: what will you know that
      you did not know already?   19

Chapter 2   The core issue – the unexpected is inevitable   **22**

2.1   Some preliminary questions   22
2.2   Two sources of the unexpected   23
2.3   How will you respond to the unexpected?   27
2.4   Cumulative consequence explored   29
2.5   Acquiescing in inefficiency   35
2.6   Be on the lookout for signals   41
2.7   Summarizing so far ...   43
2.8   An obstacle course   44
2.9   Some more questions   49

Chapter 3   Attitudes and the unexpected   **51**

3.1   Setting the tone   51
3.2   Awareness, reflection and the management
      of expectations   53
3.3   Challenge your expectations   57
3.4   Some risks of categorization   60

3.5   Good leadership or good luck?   63
3.6   Check your assumptions   64
3.7   The role of myths and stories   67
3.8   Honor the experts – wherever you find them   72
3.9   Leaders need to focus on solutions
        rather than on problems   74
3.10   Surfacing your attitudes – some key questions   75

**Chapter 4   No surprises! – anticipating and preparing
               for the unexpected   78**

4.1   Any bus can take you there   78
4.2   Doing the groundwork: personal integrity   79
4.3   Managing by exception or merely
        missing the signals?   83
4.4   Values, attitudes and beliefs   84
4.5   Doing the groundwork: organizational integrity   86
4.6   Doing the groundwork: aligning resources   92
4.7   Seeking signals, telling stories   94
4.8   How you respond to today's unexpected event
        can help prepare you for tomorrow's   99
4.9   Groundwork in summary   101
4.10   More questions   102

**Chapter 5   Understanding context – inside the
               organization: Obligations, values and
               managing paradox   104**

5.1   Formal and informal leadership obligations   104
5.2   The visible professional   106
5.3   Shaping the future: values   107
5.4   Shaping the future: visions and acts of faith   114
5.5   Paradox and unreasonable truths   117
5.6   Some more questions   120

**Chapter 6   Marshalling resources – building and
               managing commitment   122**

6.1   Different ways of thinking: engagement
        and commitment   122
6.2   Rational-analytical thinking   123
6.3   Imaginative-emotional thinking   129
6.4   Toolkits and snakepits   131

6.5	Integrated thinking	134
6.6	How well do you know your business?	134
6.7	How well do you know your people?	139
6.8	How well do you know your stakeholders?	144
6.9	Building commitment	146
6.10	Integrated thinking: leadership and trust	147

Chapter 7	**Context is key**	**150**
7.1	Keeping in touch with the external context	150
7.2	The external context: 2015?	153
7.3	The external context – competitors and suppliers	159
7.4	Sensitivity to external signals	160
7.5	Keeping in touch with the internal context: process	163
7.6	Representations of the internal context	164
7.7	Stuff goes right on happening	169
7.8	Making changes that work	170
7.9	Pulling the threads together	174

Chapter 8	**Securing the ladder – preparing**	
	your action plan	**179**
8.1	By way of introduction	179
8.2	Make time for reflection	180
8.3	Hold up and look into the mirror	181
8.4	Check the tone of your organization	182
8.5	People	183
8.6	Make changes that work	184
8.7	Articulate the changing context	186
8.8	Speed is a core competence	187
8.9	Articulate your values and your touchstones	187

Notes	189
Index	192

2.1	An ill wind?	28
2.2	Spot the deliberate mistake	30
2.3.1	How to appoint directors	36
2.3.2	Watching for his lips to move	37
2.4	The call center project	39
2.5	Symptoms of hubris?	46
3.1	Tackling the right problem?	54
3.2	Business as usual?	59
3.3	A CEO's experience of a takeover bid by a major shareholder	62
3.4	Consistent messages?	68
4.1	Remember who you are!	79
4.2	Dancing on hot coals	81
4.3	Do you need a crisis?	85
4.4	Mistakes are made by people – not by procedures	87
4.5	Who was the doctor?	95
4.6	Fire! Fire!	100
5.1	Identifying your values	109
5.2	Credit crunch values	111
5.3	Values 1	112
5.4	Values 2	113
5.5	Values on the line	115
5.6	Recurrent paradox	119
6.1	The operations director's nightmare	127
6.2	Rethinking the business 1	135
6.3	Rethinking the business 2	137
6.4	Is everyone on board?	140
6.5	Taking people decisions	143
6.6	Growth at all costs	145
7.1	A post-credit-crunch world	155

LIST OF FIGURES

7.1	The organizational pyramid	164
7.2	A classic organogram	164
7.3	Flatter structures, reduced hierarchies	165
7.4	The organization in two dimensions	165
7.5	A bird's eye organogram?	166
7.6	Some typical networks of a CEO	168

ACKNOWLEDGMENTS

Much of this book is concerned with asking questions. It could not have been written had not Geoff Armstrong, Paul Breach, Mike Brown, James Espey, George Gater, Michael Hind, Mike Kirkman, Jeremy Meyrick-Jones and, above all, John Harris permitted me to ask them impertinent questions over the course of several years as each of them addressed the consequences of unexpected events impacting themselves and their organizations. In John's case, the questioning process went on as we wrote the book together and continues to the present day.

My thanks are due to them all, as well as to Arie de Geus and Peter Honey who generously read and commented on early versions of the text, to Stephen Rutt and the team at Palgrave who have knocked it into shape and to my wife, Sandra, without whose encouragement I would not have completed my research and who frequently reminds me that answers are important too.

Graham Robinson

Over the years I have been immensely lucky to meet and work with many wonderful people who, by either being a role model or by giving me their time, have shown me how to get the best out of myself and others. There have been so many that it is impossible to thank them all by name, but I would especially like to single out Norman Roberts, Ronnie Pickering and Peter Shaw.

Huge thanks must go to Graham for his patience, great ideas and hard work; without him there would be no book and to Stephen Rutt and all at Palgrave for their encouragement and guidance.

Finally in addition to thanking all my family for their guidance and support, I must give special thanks to my grandmother. She handled the most unexpected event of her life with stoicism, courage and love and gave me my enduring values.

John Harris

CHAPTER 1

Introductions and a problem

1.1   What's the big idea?

Just who is responsible for the current mess in which we find ourselves? People like us; like you and like me. That's uncomfortable.

Just before we finished writing this book in December 2008, the world's banking system was edging back from the brink of collapse with what looked like the reluctant assistance of governments. Several leading banks did not make it. Stock markets tumbled one day, recovered the next while the dollar and the pound weakened against the euro before the pound went on to weaken against both. A global recession, if not a fully fledged slump, was imminent. Business leaders (especially bankers) were held in ever decreasing esteem as credit dried up and company after company from Wall Street to Main Street was driven to the wall. Numerous pundits appeared in the world's media to declare that what was happening had been entirely predictable. Yet many company boards, their CEOs and directors seem to have been taken completely by surprise and suffered the consequences.

Bankers at the center of the storm denied that they had any responsibility for the crisis in which we all now find ourselves. Both Richard Fuld, the former chief executive of Lehman Brothers, when questioned by a congressional committee, and Adam Applegarth, who had been CEO at the UK's Northern Rock bank, when quizzed by a group of British MPs, claimed that the circumstances that caused both banks to fail could not have been predicted. Therefore, they concluded, they were in no way responsible for what had happened. Fuld stated that night after sleepless night he had racked his brain to see if he could think of anything that he might have done differently and said that he could think of nothing. Applegarth made similar claims to the effect that what had happened had been totally beyond his control.

So why, we wonder, had Fuld been seeking to find a buyer for Lehman Brothers in the weeks before it went bust?

One of Applegarth's questioners expressed incredulity at his protestation that the crisis could not have been foreseen, since the committee on which this MP served had been discussing its likelihood for the previous six weeks.

Hindsight is a wonderful thing and, as Nick Cohen wrote in his analysis of the crisis in the Observer on 25 January 2009, "after a deluge, nothing seems as remote as the day before it came." It now is quite clear that symptoms signaling the impending fall were certainly around long before the consequences of grossly imprudent lending and the "securitization of toxic debt" had started to bite and the banks began to crumble. But little attention was paid to such signals by those who claimed to have broken the boom and bust cycle as their bonus levels rose to unprecedented heights. The business world as a whole appeared to be taken by surprise as the leaders of banks around the world realized too late what was happening and lost their nerve like rabbits caught in the headlights as the credit crunch began to bite.

We believe that being caught out by unexpected events is not particularly unusual and is in fact commonplace at the top of a great many organizations. We also believe that "unexpected events" are inevitable (whether on the scale of the banking crisis of 2008 or as individual and as personal as a redundancy, a serious illness or an accident). But we think that being taken by surprise by such events is far from inevitable. Though the details may be unpredictable or unknown, the fact that the unexpected will occur can be anticipated and prepared for so that we are not taken by surprise when it does.

It is unlikely that many of us make our best decisions or perform to the best of our capabilities when we are surprised and in a state of shock. Those who do perform well in the face of the unexpected do so because they are well prepared for it.

Despite not knowing what form unexpected events will take they do not allow themselves to be taken by surprise.

Many business leaders – respected and otherwise – have reached the top of their chosen career ladder without having taken the trouble to ensure that the ladder has been properly secured. They may be fine for years and then something happens that appears to be totally beyond their control and the ladder comes crashing down. Subsequent investigation reveals that the crash was far from inevitable and that, if they had taken the trouble to make sure that their career ladder was secure, they might well still be sitting on top of it.

You need to prepare for the unexpected because, one day, it is going to hit you!

In this book we show how those at the top of the ladder as leaders of their business or organization can prepare for unexpected events – and it is worth noting that such events are not always negative. They can just as well provide you with a great opportunity as they can confront you with a potential disaster. But, either way, if you let them take you by surprise you are much less likely to be able to deal with them appropriately.

How can you prepare for the unexpected?

- By being aware of the personal values that shape your behavior and your responses to the unexpected; the boundaries to them and how they both focus and constrain your actions.
- By identifying and articulating certain fixed points or touchstones that, for you, are unchanging and unchangeable.
- By developing your understanding of and keeping in touch with the wider context within which you are operating and by recognizing its instability – it is constantly shifting and changing.
- By learning to be comfortable while operating in an environment that is characterized by ambiguity, contradiction and paradox.

In the book we explore some of the ways in which those who are leaders of their business or other organization, or who aspire to such positions, can develop their skills and capabilities in each of these areas in order to meet the challenges that are presented to them when the unexpected occurs.

But first we should introduce ourselves.

1.2   Who we are

The book came about when the two of us, having spent much of our working lives as company directors and as advisers to others in such roles, began to ask each other questions about just what it was that we thought we were doing; what we felt we had learned from the experience of doing it and what kind of sense we now made of it.

John trained as an engineer and worked in the petrochemicals industry in a variety of roles before becoming a director of a major energy company – first of engineering, next of operations – then as managing director of the UK company and, finally, its group chief executive. He currently acts as a mentor to other directors and senior managers and consults on management and leadership matters to organizations such as UK Sport.

Graham has had a varied career – as a business-school academic, as HR director in a multinational computer company and as the director of a business development consultancy. He has now returned to writing and research work, as a visiting research fellow at the Centre for Management Learning and Development at the University of Surrey, having recently completed a six-month trip around Scandinavia and Eastern Europe – "purely for pleasure." He is the author of two other books and of numerous journal articles on organization and management matters.

1.3   For whom are we writing this book?

This is a book for people who are at, close to or on their way toward the top of their organizational ladder.

Today's organizational leaders are confronted by unprecedented levels of political, economic, social and technical uncertainty and complexity, in a world in which the occurrence of unexpected events is par for the course. While the pace of change has rarely if ever been greater, levels of regulation have also increased enormously. In the wake of the 2008 crisis in the global banking and financial services industries, the desire for greater regulation of the finance sector, dormant for 20 or more years, is definitely back. While the levels of material reward associated with organizational leadership may have been unrealistically high – and, as such, subject to both criticism and envy – the risks to health, self-esteem and personal well-being and reputation associated with providing such leadership, always considerable, are also greater than ever.

Paradoxically, this state of affairs has come about at a time when levels of formal, managerial qualification and knowledge possessed by or available to business leaders are much higher than they ever were in the past. Moreover, the range, availability of and accessibility to the kinds of information and technical tools by means of which leaders may be helped to lead and manage their organizations is also greater now than at any time previously.

Thus, while complexity, uncertainty and the pace of change have all increased dramatically, so too have the levels of knowledge, the volume of information, the range of techniques and the availability of advice and, therefore, the diversity of choice between different ways in which the issues that arise from complexity, change and uncertainty may be addressed.

However, it has been suggested that many leaders have long since reached a point of knowledge saturation or information overload. For example, some of the financial services, securities-based products that contributed to the crisis in the global banking system in the latter part of 2008 are said to have been so complex that the top management of the banks who traded in them had little or no understanding of the products that their staff were trading on their behalf, nor of the possible implications of such trading. However, while they generated huge profits for the shareholders of these institutions and colossal bonuses for their directors, managers and staff, there was little incentive to those shareholders or directors who should have been holding them to account to understand them, question them, or to rein them in.

As one commentator put it, the banking non-executive director or chief executive who had attempted to apply the brakes would have been "eaten alive by his shareholders and board members", who would have been appalled at the prospect of losing their piece of the action.

In a nutshell, business leaders have to confront a world of excessive complexity, uncertainty and change with an overloaded armory of information and a bewildering array of choices, often conflicting, between different though still relevant areas of knowledge and technique with which to tackle them. At the same time they appear to be under enormous pressure from their peers, from markets and from the media to do things that in other circumstances they might never have considered doing.

For the most part we, the authors, have thoroughly enjoyed our time as company directors – though we freely acknowledge that we have had our own periods of self-doubt and damagingly high levels of stress and anxiety while in the role. But we also recognize that a good deal of this was almost certainly avoidable and self-inflicted – for hindsight is indeed a wonderful thing. Even so, we still believe that it really is possible to operate successfully at a high level in a modern organization, enjoy a high quality of life, personal satisfaction and pleasure and still emerge with one's integrity, reputation and health intact. Moreover, we do not equate quality of life with lifestyle or with what is sometimes tellingly described as material "compensation."

So, as we stated at the beginning of this chapter, we are writing for people who are actively engaged in managerial, business organizational and leadership matters, every day of their lives. We see our readers as likely to have been quite recently appointed directors or senior managers or as people, perhaps, who aspire to fill such roles but who may be questioning the personal costs that they may incur should they do so – people, in other words, who are at or who are close to the top of the organizational ladder.

At the same time, we did not want to offer you yet another book on "how to manage" or on "how to become a successful leader." We are writing for you as the whole, complicated and endlessly intriguing individual that you are, rather than addressing you simply as a director, manager – the wearer of the label or badge that is associated with the particular role that you happen to occupy or may find yourself occupying soon in your chosen work organization.

In a single phrase, this book is for people whose heads are above the parapet and who intend to lead interesting and satisfying lives in and beyond the boardroom and its demands.

1.4   Four areas of leadership choice and challenge

Such choices may be grouped into four broad areas. The first of these – structures and standards, processes and procedures – might be regarded as being essentially logical, rational and internal to the organization. The choice concerns the way that you, as leader of your organization, decide to develop its strategies and arrange or design its structure to deliver them. It also involves developing the various processes (both complex and straightforward) by means of which your organization delivers its products and services to its customers or clients so as to achieve its stated aims and objectives.

This area tends to be formal, and is typically communicated in writing and in a familiar and replicable format, for example, through board papers, business plans, financial reports, organization charts, project management manuals, risk assessments etc. It is very much the area of standards, rules, procedure and technique and tends to involve a formal and stylized "language" that serves to emphasize its objectivity and rationality. It can, however, degenerate into the formulae, jargon and "management-speak" that are quite rightly derided as being largely devoid of real meaning. Such language often provides a major obstacle to genuine (i.e. meaningful) communication.

The second area – culture and values – has received much attention from consultants and business school academics over the past 20 years or so. Here, the focus of attention is on the ways in which people identify with the organization and relate to its leaders, formally and informally, both on and off the job. It concerns what it "means" to be a part of, say, Apple, Goldman Sachs, a Virgin company, Marks and Spencer, the John Lewis Partnership, Starbucks or a Civil Service Department, a hospital or school.

Recognizing this area's importance, the leaders of many companies and public sector organizations have gone to considerable lengths in their attempts to articulate the values that are said to be shared by members of their organizations. These have then been captured in statements that hang proudly in their reception areas, are included in their annual reports and are circulated to their employees. Such statements usually emphasize the importance of the customer and the employee, a commitment to excellence, to innovation, sustainability, shareholder value and good corporate citizenship.

We suspect that most such statements might better be described as aspirations rather than as values, and there is nothing wrong with that. However, we cannot help but note that there is a remarkable degree of similarity between the statements that are used to capture the values claimed to be held by quite different organizations in totally different lines of business activity. It is our contention that an organization's shared values are revealed in the ways in which its members behave every day, in good times and in bad; in how their actions represent the organization to their colleagues, to their customers and to the world, rather than by the value statements that hang on their walls. This is because the language of values is essentially an emotional one that is primarily used orally and informally among and between relatively small groups of people and which helps to differentiate them from other such groups.

An organization's underlying values are critical elements in its capacity for success or failure. Their language is one that tunes into people's emotions, their commitment and confidence. It may be inspirational and passionate, tired and depressed or harsh and aggressive. We have encountered quite a few organizations in which the predominant tone was harsh and aggressive but have never met one in which this was reflected in the statement of values that hung over the desk of its CEO, although we recognize that some macho chief executives come pretty close to doing so.

For example, Dick Fuld, former chief executive of the collapsed bank Lehman Brothers, was apparently nicknamed The Gorilla. Quite happy with this name and the image it conveyed, Fuld is said to have had a stuffed gorilla seated in a chair in his office. Furthermore he communicated the values symbolized by the animal in many of his verbal communications. He is alleged to have stated that, "when I find a short-seller, I want to tear his heart out and eat it before his eyes while he is still alive." Such values, as we shall see, went on to be shared throughout the bank.

If you saw trouble ahead, how happy would you be to point this out to a gorilla with such culinary tastes?

The third area – organizational leadership style – is clearly closely related to the second. This again involves your behavior and the manner in which it reflects the style and quality of leadership that you offer to the organization and its stakeholders in your leadership role. But in this case the focus is upon your personal behavior and style as an individual. We do not suggest that there is any one, "best" style of leadership. What is appropriate will depend on circumstance, situation and context and upon even more tenuous, less tangible factors, such as your "character", breadth of vision and the personal touchstones to which your aspirations are anchored. So, while we would never claim that there is any one "best" style of leadership, we would certainly maintain that the consistency of your leadership style is very important indeed.

This area takes us into the realms of ethics and morality. We hold that organizational leadership is essentially a moral activity and that the language of leadership reflects this, emphasizing the beliefs, the personal vision and the expectations of commitment that those in leadership roles have of other people and which in turn other people may have of those who lead them.

The fourth and final area of leadership choice and challenge – self-awareness – is the most personal and private of them all, since it concerns your sense of self, your motives and drivers; your capacity for self-insight, your sense of self-belief and self-worth and your own set of personal capabilities – in essence, what it is that makes you the unique individual that you are.

The "language" involved here is that of the inner dialog that takes place within your head. As such it is directly accessible by you and by nobody else.

Your presence at the top of a twenty-first century organization requires you to be able to function effectively (this also means "appropriately") in each one of these areas simultaneously. The newly appointed chief executive, once the initial euphoria of being appointed has worn off, might be forgiven for thinking that he or she requires the intellectual and rational problem-solving capacity of an Einstein, the ability to "be the brand" of a Richard Branson, the leadership capability of a Henry the fifth at Agincourt and the moral integrity and self-awareness of the Dalai Lama. This really is quite a challenge. A challenge that involves the ability to balance different sets of demands that are frequently contradictory or in conflict, while maintaining a steady course in pursuit of the goals that you have set for yourself and for the organization that you lead.

1.5   A major issue: why would you want to be a leader?

An unfortunate consequence of a wider recognition of the nature of this challenge, coupled with an increasingly jaded view of business leaders on the part of the general public, appears to be that increasing numbers of people with much needed levels of knowledge, skill and leadership potential are choosing to opt out of organizational life altogether. As we began writing this book, the media were informing us that there is a scarcity of applicants in the UK for positions as head teachers and senior National Health Service and other public sector managers. While in the private sector too, many executives are questioning the impact that their managerial and leadership positions is having upon their quality of life. Increasingly, many are opting to "downshift", questioning their work-life balance and choosing alternative ways in which to live their lives. The pressures and risks associated with many leadership roles are such that well-qualified potential candidates are simply unwilling to put themselves forward to undertake them, notwithstanding the high levels of reward that have been on offer to them for doing so.

Such reward levels, particularly in the financial services sector, have become the object of increasing public criticism, being regarded as symbolizing rampant greed rather than as recognition for challenging jobs that have been well done. Despite this, the leaders of several of the banks that were baled out by their governments in 2008 and 2009 attracted further ignominy by seeming to believe that they should continue to pay out large bonuses, now funded to a large extent from the public purse, to prevent the brilliant staff who had designed the systems that had brought them to their knees from going elsewhere. Presumably the "elsewhere" they had in mind did not, as one wag suggested, include prison. After all they had done nothing illegal; their actions were merely incompetent and immoral.

We would suggest, in the light of the revelations that have followed the crisis in banking, that remuneration levels have become ends in themselves, leading to inadequate attention being given to the means of their achievement.

But it is still argued that the very high reward levels enjoyed by those at the top reflect the market rate for these leadership roles. This may well be true. Yet, nearly 50 years ago, Frederick Herzberg pointed out that, beyond a certain point, satisfaction levels do not go up significantly or sustainably as pay increases. Quite the contrary, pay becomes an active source of dissatisfaction when it is compared with that of peers or rivals. It is what it symbolizes that matters rather than the pay level itself. "Does what I am paid suggest that I am I keeping ahead, or am I falling behind my peers and rivals?" One more thing to be anxious about.

Generally speaking, our levels of relative affluence, compared with the experiences of our parents and grandparents, means that working in order to live rather than living in order to work had, before the credit crunch kicked in, become a genuine rather than a hypothetical choice for a great many people. But over the past 10 or 15 years it became distinctly unfashionable to exercise this choice. The pressure "to have rather than to be" has been enormous as is starkly described by Oliver James in his book Affluenza.[1] The personal consequences of an apparent pursuit of money for its own sake has been quite startling. Thus, we have been encouraged to work excessively long hours in exchange for the opportunity to acquire a level of bonus income that enables us to purchase a lifestyle that would be truly enjoyable if only we had the time to pursue it. Having a mansion, yacht and Mediterranean villa that we rarely get to use is not the point; it is what our possessing them says about us that appears to be important.

But even before the onset of the credit crunch worms appeared to be starting to turn.

We began the conversations that led to this book back in 2006 when the global economy was still booming. One of the questions that we posed to ourselves was, "Why is it that more and more people who have invested so much time and effort in climbing the organizational ladder appear to be opting to get off before they reach the top?" Other questions we asked ourselves were, "Why do so many people, who have reached the top of the ladder, fall off once they do get there?" and "Why is it that so many people who have reached the top seem to be so unhappy with their lot?"

Perhaps people were opting to downshift simply because their affluence, as compared with that of previous generations of business leaders and managers made it possible for them to do so. Or perhaps it was a natural response to the spate of cases of serious corporate malfeasance that became public in cases such as Enron in recent years. Oliver James suggests that we are witnessing the effects of a seriously damaging social virus that has been undermining the health of our communities, especially in the English-speaking nations, where the race to the top has become much more one of gaining a comparative advantage in image and a desire for celebrity than one of leading, let alone of serving. Might it be that the desire of contestants in The Apprentice to appear on TV and to become celebrities considerably outweighed their professed wish to get to lead a successful business?

But now in the midst of a global recession many more people are finding themselves "downshifting", not as a matter of personal choice but as a consequence of unexpected events by which some people will be devastated but which others will seize upon for the opportunity to make a life change for which they had previously lacked the confidence to take voluntarily.

1.6 More challenges

1.6.1 Don't let the unexpected catch you unprepared!

A great many challenges are involved in successfully leading an organization at any time. During an economic downturn, recession or slump these challenges are greatly augmented.

The challenges that we have outlined were around long before the present understandable preoccupation with the instability of the world's banking system and consequent global recession developed. We have already noted that the world is becoming more complex, more uncertain and we have suggested four, interdependent areas of complexity within which organizational leaders need to be able to operate with both competence and confidence if they are to be effective. We have also noted that each area has its own, slightly different, "language."

So, the challenge of functioning effectively in each of these four areas simultaneously is not limited to their individual complexity or to that of the relationships that exist between them. Each requires a different form of communication while simultaneously needing a communication process that is equally accessible to all who are involved in it. This process depends on the possession of a set of very unusual skills on the part of those in positions of leadership who must ensure that these different areas are integrated effectively. These skills involve communicating meaningfully and convincingly in what are in effect quite different specialist languages in ways that enable different interest groups to unite in the pursuit of a set of common causes.

In addition, each one of our four areas is increasingly subject to the impact of significant events that appear to come out of the blue and which are largely unexpected.

The attitudes that organizational leaders display toward such events are crucial to the organization's capacity to respond to them and to manage their consequences. Unfortunately, the attitudes of such leaders may be the cause of some of these unexpected events, especially if they are unsure of, or are not in touch with, the personal characteristics that determine the manner in which they lead and respond to such events when they do occur.

In the book, we explore what appear to us to be the requirements of leadership in managing the unexpected. We stress the fundamental importance of preparation if the unexpected is not to catch the leader by surprise and offguard. We believe that one reason for increasing numbers of organizational leaders to fall from the summit of their previously seemingly secure career ladders may be found in the ways in which they have responded to the impact of unexpected events. Such responses tend to reflect some or all of the following:

- Inadequate preparation
- Inappropriate behavior, language and communication
- Limited self-insight and awareness
- Failure to keep in touch with context

While some unexpected events and their negative consequences are truly unavoidable, we are concerned that too many others are the consequence of avoidable error – either way; the likelihood of their occurring could and should have been anticipated.

For example, when John was working in petrochemicals, matters of health and safety were always of paramount consideration. "In our industry you would no more walk past an unsecured ladder than take a bungee jump without making quite sure that the rope was properly attached." Yet, time and time again, just as we meet people who see health and safety matters as a nuisance, an obstacle placed by overzealous bureaucrats in the way of their achieving what they are paid to achieve, we encounter people in positions of organizational leadership who have not taken the time or the trouble to ensure that the career ladder on the top of which they are perched has been properly secured. Such people are most at risk when the unexpected happens. It catches them unprepared, often meaning that the actions that they take are ineffective, making bad matters worse or causing them to fail to capitalize upon major opportunities.

1.7   Obligations and key messages

1.7.1   Anticipate the unexpected

We intend to show that it is perfectly possible to derive high value from the impact of the unexpected, provided that you have recognized its inevitability (though you will never know its details in advance), that you are well prepared and that, when it happens, the responses that you make are appropriate. This may seem blindingly obvious but experience tells us that, while formalized, risk management and disaster-recovery processes make a vitally important contribution, the climate and tone of the organization that you set, together with the levels of personal anticipation and preparedness that are revealed in the ways that you behave as the organization's leader are just as critical. It is these personal factors that can make the difference between your performance at the top being heroic or tragic.

We believe that leading an organization, no matter what its size, carries with it certain obligations. Some of these obligations are fairly obvious and are routinely set out in management and leadership texts. But all too often the obvious is taken for granted simply because it is obvious. Such obligations include articulating the organization's vision, its goals and objectives. Others though are more subtle, such as setting the "tone" of the organization and then being aware of the tone that you have set and of its impact; living the organization's values (rather than merely publishing them); understanding the people and processes upon which the organization's and your own success depend; securing and building the commitment of others; staying in touch with the wider context within which your business operates and, perhaps above all, understanding yourself, the touchstones in terms of which you operate and the boundaries that you will never, ever cross.

As an organizational leader, you are the guardian and champion of integrity – your own and that of the organization, and you are likely to find that your integrity will be tested – regularly. You are also the keeper and champion of your organization's mission, purpose and values. This obligation goes way beyond published mission statements, goals, objectives and targets. This is because the gap between an organization's stated mission and values as aspirations and the ways in which its directors, managers and employees behave toward one another and toward their customers and other stakeholders is often so wide as to devalue their currency.

1.7.2   Shape the future, stay in touch with context

As leader of your organization, you are under an obligation to shape its future, taking into account the myriad contextual fluctuations, opportunities and changes that you will encounter as you guide it towards the particular vision of the future that you have articulated. Therefore, the ability to stay in touch with context is a critical obligation of an organization's leaders and is a key determinant of any organization's future success.

We think that the recent infatuation with highly focused targets, as has been, for example, particularly evident on the part of UK government ministers has often backfired and undermined the achievement of the organization's overall purpose. Highly specific, quantifiable targets have often caused people, not only at the top but at all organizational levels, to narrow their span of attention and to lose touch with the wider context within which they operate. Concentrating excessively on the bottom line at the expense of future quality in the private sector is another example; increasing hospital bed occupancy at the expense of infection control and focusing the attention of schoolteachers on league tables at the expense of pupil's enthusiasm for learning provide further, public sector, illustrations. All too often measurable targets seem to us to have existed primarily because of their measurability rather than because of their overall contribution to the achievement of an organization's purpose, significance and quality. In addition people whose attention has been overly focused on the achievement of targets have become increasingly vulnerable to the impact of unplanned and unexpected events.

1.7.3   Performing the juggling act

Meeting these obligations isn't a matter of having had the relevant education and training, acquired the knowledge and built up the experience that will enable you to "know" the right answers when you need them. Of course these may be important factors, each contributing to you and your organization's success or otherwise. We readily acknowledge that what you have done in the past is a critical factor in determining what you are able to do now, often enabling you to draw upon knowledge that you didn't know you had (or had forgotten that you ever possessed) when you need it. Of course, some of your past experiences are going to be significant in enabling you to ask the right questions of those who are required to manage the detail, deliver against targets and get things done; helping them to ensure that what they are doing is still appropriate in circumstances of change and uncertainty, or in assisting them to take the risk of doing something new and different when it is not.

This involves you in an important balancing or juggling act. On the one hand it involves asking a set of questions, the answers to which will keep you on top of the detailed processes upon which the organization depends if it is to deliver against its mission, purpose and aims. On the other hand, you also need to be asking the kinds of questions that will keep you abreast of the shifts and adjustments in the organization's climate that will occur as it reacts and responds to the impact of unexpected events that shape the context, the bigger picture within which you and your organization must function.

To perform this balancing act successfully requires the ability on your part as a leader to stop, to reflect and to question, asking yourself, for example, "How would I respond in similar circumstances to this opportunity or to that crisis?" It is just as important to have the confidence and courage to hold up the mirror in order to be able to assure yourself that the answer you give is an honest one, one from which you can learn and on which you may build.

1.8   How to use the book

1.8.1   "A book to keep by you and to dip into … every now and then"

We shall return frequently to the importance of asking questions, but will not waste your time by providing you with our answers to them. In our view a book that attempted to provide the answers to the kinds of questions that leaders need to be asking themselves when confronted by unexpected events would almost certainly miss the point. It is you who need to be asking yourself the questions that are relevant and appropriate to the particular circumstances in which you find yourself, taking into account the nature and qualities of the unique person that you are.

While we do not advocate reinventing the wheel, developing a deep insight into your own particular context and situation is much more important than reading the answers that someone else, who is not you, has provided to similar questions in different circumstances, in a different location and at another time. Your own answers are the ones that matter, since these are the ones that will determine the actions that you will take.

So, many of the issues that we raise will be associated with questions to you of the kind:

"What would you do in circumstances like these?"

Please note, we are not asking the question, "What would you like to have done?" That is a very different matter, and likely to produce answers that reveal your aspirations and your good intentions rather than what you would actually do when the chips are down, you are under pressure, in unfamiliar circumstances and with people whose motives and capabilities may be uncertain or unknown to you.

When you are truly honest with yourself it is more likely that the answers that you provide to the question – "What would you do?" – will reflect the ways that you really would act in practice, difficult though it may be sometimes for you to accept what such answers tell you about yourself. However, responding honestly to such questions in advance of the unexpected happening greatly increases the chance that you will limit the damage that you sustain when it does.

Our wish is that this should be the kind of book that you will keep by you and continue to use, dipping into it every now and then in order to stimulate your own self-questioning. Not out of self-doubt but as part of a continuous process of learning, developing and staying in touch with a world that is subject to constant uncertainty and change. Of course, there's no harm in reading the book straight through – we hope that you will enjoy its combination of conversations, stories, reflections and questions; however you choose to read and use it.

1.9 If you read this book: what will you know that you did not know already?

1.9.1 "All of us know a great deal more than we know that we know, or than we think that we know"

We hope that by asking yourself the kinds of questions that we pose in the book and through providing your own answers to them, you will increase your ability to anticipate the unexpected, to recognize opportunities, problems and their possible solutions as they arise and to address them both appropriately and successfully.

We hope that you will get to know, really know, yourself better and that you may come to be at ease with, while continuing to be challenged by, what you learn.

Of course we do not know the people who will pick up or read this book. However, unlike the former US Defense Secretary Donald Rumsfeld, we are utterly convinced that all of us know a great deal more than we know that we know, or than we think that we know. Neither do we always know how we know what we know. We are also convinced that all of us know a great deal more than we are able to fully articulate. This may limit our ability to pass on what we know to others. Much gets lost in translation between the different languages that we employ in addressing the various areas of decision choice with which we are confronted.

We believe that your responses to the kinds of questions raised by the book will place you in a better position from which to develop and use the kind of language that is necessary to integrate these decision choices and their outcomes effectively to the benefit of the organization that you lead.

Perhaps in the end it really is largely down to experience, practice and intuition. But leading an organization and dealing with the unexpected occurrences that are the inevitable companions of the role of an organizational leader, requires you to be able to draw on such tacit knowledge effectively and with confidence. It also requires you to acknowledge that it is not simply a matter of luck and your natural, personal brilliance – it takes preparation, anticipation and practice. It also demands that you take time out for reflection. When you are under pressure and when time is a scarce and precious commodity, such necessary reflection can easily become an early casualty, increasing the extent to which you are at risk of falling from your career ladder.

Through reading and reflecting on this book we believe that you can assist yourself to meet the challenge of successfully performing the balancing act that can enable you to manage the detail without being swamped by it, and to stay in touch with context without being carried away or paralyzed by its uncertainties.

1.9.2   Why on earth did I do that?

During the course of carrying out the research upon which parts of the book are based, the directors who were interviewed frequently made observations of the following kind:

> I cannot understand why I did what I did. I knew that the outcome would be (a) when I wanted (b) but under pressure and in the heat of the moment I went for (a). Looking back on it I can't believe that I did that!

or:

> When it happened, I seemed to go onto autopilot. I knew
> instinctively what I had to do and did it. You might say it was
> an act of blind faith, but I just knew that it was what had to
> be done, and so it proved.

We want this book to be a help to you in thinking about how
you will deal with the unexpected events that you will encounter
in the future as a leader of your organization and we hope that
you will be satisfied with your responses to the questions that
it poses.

CHAPTER 2

The core issue – the unexpected is inevitable

2.1 Some preliminary questions

Why are so many highly experienced and competent leaders caught out and taken by surprise by unexpected events for which they are unprepared, with the consequence that they then do things that seriously damage their organizations and themselves? Why do they fail to notice the alarm signals that are so often shown to have been sounding long before the specific event that did them so much harm actually occurred? What was it that during 2008 caused the leaders of many of the world's long-established and highly respected financial institutions to lead these institutions to self-destruction, dragging the global economy down with them?

As leader of your organization you will be aware that you are expected to take charge, to be proactive and make things happen in line with your goals, your plans and your objectives. If you fail to do this, your tenure of office will be brief. But you cannot afford to fall into the trap of thinking that, just because you are in charge, you are in control. Of course, you cannot afford to be out of control, but you need to accept the limits that there are to the extent to which control is possible. As leader you ride an unstable charger in an environment characterized by change and uncertainty. If you have recently arrived at the top of your organization by means of promotion from inside the organization, both the organization and its relationship with its environment will now be different, since your arrival at the top is a significant change in itself. If, on the other hand, your success in one organization has led to your being placed in charge of another, that organization too will have changed in tone, in values and patterns of behavior as a consequence of your arrival.

2.1.1 "Stuff happens"

The experience of managing a company in the current business climate has been compared to that of white-water rafting. This metaphor was never so appropriate as when the first decade of the twenty-first century began to draw to a close. So, although you may be planning to get from "A" to "B", you know that the journey is going to be bumpy, unpredictable and carrying a significant degree of risk. Such risk may well be part what attracted you to the position of leader in the first place. The days of stable bureaucracies, much derided but remarkably successful in their time, even if somewhat dull, are over. For years it has been suggested that the only certainties in life are death and taxes and, more recently, that "stuff happens".

But the way that you respond to such "stuff" is one very important determinant of your leadership qualities and, therefore, of the level of success that you will achieve.

Let's assume for a moment that you are a newly appointed chief executive. Your arrival at the top is unsettling, both for you and for your organization. Almost certainly you will have to adjust your expectations, since pretty soon you will need to contend with occurrences that were not in your brief – unexpected events.

2.2 Two sources of the unexpected

What exactly do we mean by an unexpected event? The American writers and business academics Karl Weick and Kathleen Sutcliffe suggest that an unexpected event can be said to have occurred, "when expected strategy and performance outcomes fail to materialize or when unexpected impediments to strategy and performance outcomes materialize."[1] So far, so good. But we believe that such unexpected events may be usefully divided into two further important categories.

2.2.1   "the genuine ..."

The first of these we would describe as being genuine. They are produced by happenings over which you, as an organizational leader, have absolutely no influence or control. They may occur either inside the boundaries of your organization or beyond them in the organization's wider environment. In either case things can happen, quite out of the blue, that were not in the plan but with whose consequences you are going to have to deal. They can involve events such as the sudden drying up of credit that is a preoccupation at the time of writing, or such things as the unannounced resignation of a crucial board member (ally or opponent), the development of a material by a competitor that renders a key product-line in your business obsolete, a natural or man-made disaster (such as a plane crash or terrorist attack), the serious illness of a colleague or family member, or more positively, the windfall of the sudden demand for a product or service from a source totally outside your current market but to which you must respond. Whatever the nature of such genuinely unexpected events, you are going to have to deal with their consequences despite their not having been in the plan.

2.2.2   and the "cumulative consequence"

The second kind of unexpected event involves what we might call "events of cumulative consequence." Such events are likely to arise frequently within your sphere of influence and control unless you take active steps to prevent them. In other words, while they may appear to come out of the blue, they are in fact the direct outcome of a chain of earlier events or actions that began with something that was, ought, or could have been under your control. These are the "unsecured ladders" of our title. They can tip you from your perch at the top of your organizational ladder if you are not constantly on the lookout for the seedlings from which they may, if permitted, grow steadily until they are big enough to pull you down. They are the accidents waiting to happen. In some industries, such as petrochemicals or construction, the fact that the materials and environment involved are potentially toxic or hazardous means that matters of health and safety are always placed at the top of the agenda. In these industries, ladders that are left unsecured are recognized by all involved as the potential threats to safety that they are. The same should be true of the threats to which the career ladders of all organizational leaders are exposed. So why not subject the career that you have worked so hard to build to the same kind of risk analysis and assessment to which you subject your business strategies and deals?

Or would you prefer to accept as an article of faith the image provided by the myths surrounding you as a consequence of having made it to the top? There is a significant difference between critical self-examination and debilitating self-doubt; between justified self-confidence and, putting it bluntly, an unjustifiable belief in your own bullshit.

Both the genuinely unexpected event and those that arise as the cumulative consequence of past omissions or errors will test your capability as a leader. The first kind may be of global significance, reframing the way that we all look at the world, or they may be much more personal and closer to home. The 9/11 attacks on New York in 2001, the Boxing Day tsunami of 2004 and hurricane Katrina in 2005 were each, in their different ways, events of the first kind. Though, it could be argued and has been argued that the threat of terrorism was known before the 9/11 attacks, that the need for a global tsunami warning system had been stated prior to the tsunami that took so many lives that December and that seasonal hurricanes were by no means unfamiliar in the southern states of the US. But no business leader could have predicted the precise location, size and scope of such specific, era-defining incidents prior to the moment that they occurred. Similarly, the Asian currency crises of the mid-1990s stood the plans and strategies of many Western businesses on their heads as did the banking crisis that followed the implosion of the US subprime mortgage market in 2007/2008. The trends may have been there, but the precise timing of the tumbling of the particular financial dominos and the widespread repercussions of their collapse caught many businesses and their leaders totally by surprise.

Other recent global events have reminded many business leaders of the need to, "think global and act local", as they have been forced to respond to the local impact of the sudden surge in the rates of economic growth of the new, energy-and-raw-materials hungry giants that are India and China. It is now only too clear that climate change and global warming will be major drivers of future political, economic, technological and social instability, the outcomes of which are, for now, highly unpredictable. We could be drawn into a debate as to which of our two kinds of event might climate change be said to be. It is pretty clear that it is a cumulative consequence of human action, but not one that we think could be fairly laid at your door as a new organizational leader.

The banking crisis of 2008 and the global recession that has followed it were anticipated by many economists and others. The huge profits and individual bonuses enjoyed by many in the financial services and banking sector were clearly unsustainable. Yet some of the oldest and most highly respected players in the financial services market seemed to be taken completely by surprise when the crunch came and they either collapsed, like Lehman Brothers, or would have done so had they not, like Northern Rock and the Allied Irish Bank, been bailed out by governments fearing the imminent collapse of their nation's financial and economic systems.

How could this have come about? Is it simply an awful illustration of the triumph of hope over experience, of the leaders of formerly staid institutions being overwhelmed by greed and hubris, or is it merely the natural consequence of one more turn of the economic cycle that, though on a grander scale than predicted, was inevitable?

Whatever the answer to such questions may prove to be, as far as you, the leader of your organization, are concerned, you are going to have to deal with the impact of such events on your own business. But we should note that the critical unexpected event may be one having much less of a global impact than have those we have just described. It could be a need to revise downwards the market's expectations of your midyear profit forecast following the announcement of a breakthrough product by one of your competitors; it could be the resignation of your finance director following the diagnosis of a life-threatening heart condition; the bankruptcy of a major supplier; the need to respond to press allegations of malfeasance on the part of a key colleague or, indeed, allegations about your own conduct with which you must deal.

2.3 How will you respond to the unexpected?

The unexpected is inevitable, and its implications for you and for your company may be good or bad. But the manner in which you respond to it will be a critical factor in determining which way the outcome goes and the extent of the damage or benefit that accrues from it.

How do you respond when you discover the unethical or otherwise unacceptable behavior on the part of a key and trusted colleague on whom you have come to depend? Do you focus on the behavior and deal with it or do you make allowances for it on account of favors done or services provided in the past? When do you compromise? When do you stick to your guns and when do you make a strategic retreat in order to return even stronger at some future date? How do you determine what kinds of things might cause you to respond to such questions differently?

When we were writing this chapter, we began to worry that we were beginning to sound like two Jeremiahs, prophets of gloom and doom, pointing out the potential disasters that lurk around every corner, ready to strike at the misplaced optimism of newly appointed business leaders – "things could be worse and, lo and behold, they were!" As the world's banking and finance sector began to unravel around us, tipping us all into recession we might have been forgiven for concluding that our personal, depressing prognosis was justified. This would have missed the point.

2.3.1 Make the unexpected welcome – while accepting that it is uncomfortable

We must emphasize that the unexpected event that arrives out of the blue may just as well be offering you a golden opportunity as threatening to plunge you into crisis. The questions we pose are just as much concerned with whether or not you will be in a position to take advantage of it when such a windfall arises. Or will you, perhaps, be hamstrung by over-commitment to current plans and projects, and unable to seize the opportunity before it has already been snatched from you by a competitor?

2.1   An ill wind?

Between 2006 and 2008 the on-going political uncertainties of the Middle East and South America coupled with the surge in demand for energy from the new economies resulted in the price of oil and gas rising to previously unimagined levels. This huge rise in prices caused a great many minds to focus on the need to reduce our dependence on and consumption of carbon dioxide producing fossil fuels. The price-rises and threats to supply concentrated minds far more effectively than had the campaigns of those who had been warning of the threat to the planet that was posed by global warming. This suggests that, before we will willingly overcome our inherent levels of inertia in order to move out of our comfort zones and take action, we need to be convinced that there will be a positive pay-off to us from doing so. The threat posed by global warming, though dire, seemed to have less of an impact on behavior than the large and unexpected increase in the world price of oil and threats to gas supply. Many people changed their behavior to turn to "greener" energy sources (for a while), but only when they felt the pain in their wallets and the chill in their homes.

It really is an ill wind that blows no good – as the record profits of the oil and gas companies during the same year attest. However, the reputations of these companies will not only be determined by how they and national governments respond to the genuine unexpected events that gave rise to the windfall profits generated by the unprecedented hike in energy prices and the profits that were associated with them. Nor will they depend on how they are seen to address more fundamental issues of climate change and global warming – hopefully, before it is too late. The reputations of such companies and of their incumbent leaders are just as likely to be determined by the ways that they have conducted themselves in the wake of unexpected events that are the cumulative consequence of "unsecured ladders" such as catastrophic plant failures (whether in Hemel Hempstead, UK or Texas, US), overstated oil reserves, environmental pollution, untreated pipeline corrosion, and revelations in the media concerning the private lives of their leaders. Each of which could and should have been anticipated and avoided.

Even what may appear to be the worst of bad news can have its positive outcomes, while the apparently trivial may prove catastrophic. Studies of the personal stories of managers made redundant during the downturns of the 1980s and 1990s suggest that many of them emerged from the experience feeling much more positive than did those of their colleagues who had kept their jobs (Hurst, 1995[2]; Noer, 1993[3]). Many of those who were made redundant described how, on reflection, their being out of a job forced them to take advantage of their situation and to discover and then to pursue opportunities that they might never previously have risked.

Meanwhile, many of those who remained in their organizations felt just like survivors. No longer secure and experiencing feelings of guilt that they had hung on to their jobs while respected colleagues were cast aside, they often described themselves as feeling anxious and demoralized in the posts they had retained within their downsized organizations.

We need, therefore, to be open-minded about the assumptions that are made about the consequences that will follow from an unexpected event. Every cloud will have its silver lining, while every positive change will have a painful consequence for somebody.

2.4 Cumulative consequence explored

Our second kind of unexpected event, the kind that is a "cumulative consequence", is likely to be at least as or more common than the first. In some organizations it may be a great deal more common. This is the kind of event kind that could have been anticipated and is the result of avoidable error, neglect or inadequate management. The fact that it was not dealt with is ultimately an indictment of the organization's leadership.

We have used the metaphor of the unsecured ladder in the title of the book because, for us, it illustrates a problem rife in many of the organizations that we know. It is not so much the unsecured ladder that is the problem, it is the fact that people know that the ladder is not properly secured but fail to do anything about it. Ultimately, not dealing with metaphorical unsecured ladders is a failure of leadership because it results not only in error, accident or catastrophe but in the diversion of vital managerial and organizational energies away from the attainment of planned goals.

In the previous section we noted that, quite apart from distracting you from the achievement of your goals, such diversions can also undermine your ability to take advantage of major opportunities or to respond appropriately to the genuine unexpected event that can then knock you even further off course. You may not be able to exercise complete control over the occurrence of consequential errors, but you can and must do everything in your power to keep the risk of their happening to a minimum.

Make sure that your ladders (metaphorical and in reality) are well secured, by ensuring that a sense of responsibility for making them secure is seen as a priority for every single person within your organization. Once again this is down to the leadership that you provide, rather than a matter of policy and procedure. Every day, people with responsibility for leading their organizations disregard this piece of homespun, commonsense wisdom. It is something of which nearly all of us are guilty. Why?

2.2 Spot the deliberate mistake

Many years ago, Graham participated in a management workshop conducted by one of his personal heroes, Professor Chris Argyris of Harvard University.[4] The Professor began the workshop with a question:

"Is it possible", he asked, *"to design an error or mistake? Surely, if you knowingly plan to do something (or not to do it) then, surely, what you do (or do not do) cannot properly be called a mistake."*

This question was debated for a while, until a consensus was reached that the action taken might, perhaps, have been based on false or inadequate information and, therefore, could not be said to have been designed. Argyris agreed with this, and then asked, *"But what if you had all the necessary information and knowledge and still committed the error? Would that then be a case of error by design?"* We continued to argue the toss about this for a while and then, by way of helping us out, Professor Argyris asked us a number of questions about our own organizations. For example, did we think that upward communication channels in our companies were as open as they should be? Were positive changes often thwarted by inertia on the part of those people who would have to implement them (*"we've always done things this way"*)? In general, were mistakes acknowledged or did they tend to be covered up? Did we preach co-operation and trust, but experience conflict and lack of commitment?

Almost without exception, the workshop participants indicated that the problems suggested by Argyris' questions were quite common in every one of our organizations. He then asked why we thought such problems existed so widely, when we not only recognized them but had all agreed that they were a hindrance to our organizations' levels of success.

We all acknowledged that such chronic problems existed within our organizations, and that we had the ability to deliver solutions to problems of far greater complexity than these. While we all agreed that they were dragging down the performance levels of our various companies, we also had to admit that we had all put up with them for years.

"Doesn't this mean", he suggested, *"that you are actually designing error into your organizations?"*

Everyone who attended Professor Argyris' workshop clearly recognized the problems that he described and that they seriously inhibited the performance of their organizations, yet everyone seemed to be quite content to allow them to persist, accepting them as sad facts of organizational life that we had to put up with. He concluded by pointing out a number of errors which, he suggested, are commonly to be found within a great many organisations.

He maintained that while leaders often claim that their actions are aimed at raising levels of understanding and effectiveness, in reality they generate confusion, misunderstanding and ineffectiveness. Similarly, when things go wrong we often blame other people or inadequacies in "the system" for what are in fact consequences of our own poor decisions. We tend to suffer from organizational inertia, allowing things that we consider to have been tried and tested in the past to take precedence over the innovative and imaginative when deciding what needs to be done in unfamiliar situations. Difficult issues are routinely sanitized when being communicated upwards with the result that much upward communication becomes irrelevant or ineffective, so people tend not to bother to attempt to communicate difficult issues upwards. In many organizations there is a tendency to regard the manipulation of budgets, the liberal interpretation or even the deliberate misinterpretation of policy and procedure, together with personal political manoeuvring as things to be tolerated as inevitable facts of organizational life. He suggested that when it suits our plans or arguments we are quite likely to make the assumption that people will act in ways that we perceive to be rational when our experience tells us that this is in fact quite unlikely. We refer to our senior colleagues and others around us as our "team", when in fact any semblance of teamwork is likely to fall apart in the face of problems that are potentially threatening or embarrassing to individuals within the so-called team.

He saved his most devastating observation until the last when he said, "the worst error of all is to recognize that such things are errors. If they exist they persist and if they persist they have been around for a long time and must be being taken for granted. To take them for granted is a monumental error".

Just as was the case at the workshop, we can both think of numerous examples of such counterproductive behaviors in our own experience. Perhaps the last point in Argyris' list was the most telling: We know that these chronic problems exist in our organizations, but we allow them to persist so that they can steadily sap organizational strength, energy and creativity and, thus, seriously undermine its effectiveness.

While we believe that there is a great deal of truth in what Professor Argyris had to say, we don't think that organizational leaders deliberately set out to design the errors that make people in their organizations behave in inappropriate ways. But neither do we believe that such things, like "stuff", just happen. They are a consequence of organizational leaders losing sight of overall goals and priorities, of focusing too intently on specific projects and targets, of cutting corners and of unfulfilled good intentions to "get back to it later." The payoff from correcting such errors is perceived to be less advantageous than the pursuit and achievement of "sexier" short-term goals. So instead of dealing with them, we make allowances for them allowing them to continue to weaken our performance. Thus making mistakes by design.

2.4.1   The messages that our actions convey

Such failures convey the dangerous message that the basics have become just too basic to be of concern to us as organizational leaders, and that, therefore, they may safely be ignored, compromised or transgressed by everyone else in the organization because our attitudes suggest that they really don't matter all that much.

But, on reflection, the most depressing thing about Argyris' questions and our answers to them is that few if any of us who attended the workshop did more than nod sagely, before going back to doing nothing about the chronic issues that we had all acknowledged were inhibiting our organizations' performance.

The rot starts long before such problems reach the chronic stage and go on to generate unexpected events of cumulative consequence.

We suggest that you consider your answers to the following questions before thinking of some examples of such issues within your own experience:

- How do you deal with a colleague or senior staff member whose performance is critical to the success of the business but whose ethics trouble you?
- How do you deal with the colleague who has supported you on your journey to the top but who is no longer pulling his/her weight now that you are there?
- When required to deliver bad news, do you dress it up, put a positive spin on it and attempt to reduce its painful impact?
- How receptive are you to ideas for change or improvements offered by people who are much lower down the organization than you are?
- How do you respond to those who question your decisions or your reasons for making them?
- How do you react when a colleague or junior staff member makes a mistake?
- How would you respond to the journalist who telephones you with a request for a comment about a story of alleged wrongdoing on the part of a close colleague?
- How do you think other people might expect you to respond to such questions?

Most organizations have rules and procedures that relate to the handling of the kinds of issues that are raised by such questions. But when thinking about the penultimate question, for example, might you risk falling into the trap of allowing the media person who is questioning you to determine the agenda, rather than following the rules and procedures of your organization? After all, such a questioner is there with the objective of putting you on the spot in order to get "a good story." But that doesn't mean that you have to play by their rules, especially when you have perfectly appropriate ones of your own.

Despite this, time and again, directors and senior managers appear to forget their own rules of the game by responding to the media's questions in its terms rather than the organization's. In so doing, they make a difficult situation worse.

So here are two more questions?

- How familiar are with you with the rules, processes and procedures that are supposed to regulate behavior in your organization?
- How relevant and up-to-date are they?

2.5   Acquiescing in inefficiency

Weick and Sutcliffe's "high reliability organizations"[5] are those that have to function regularly in situations that are extremely risky. They include, for example, organizations that employ fire-fighters, lifeboat crews and those that utilize equipment where the consequences of error or failure would quite likely be catastrophic, such as in an aircraft or a petrochemical or nuclear plant.

We would be loath to board an aircraft belonging to an airline whose pilots we felt were likely to take shortcuts on their preflight checks. Because of this, airlines are careful to convey an aura of technical efficiency in everything that they do. This extends to the quasi-military style of the uniforms worn by flight attendants and ground staff. Somehow, we feel differently about a pilot of an airliner who is wearing a smart peaked-cap, a matching uniform with epaulets and winged badges than we would about one wearing a baseball cap, Bermuda shorts and a tee shirt.

Running a business is increasingly a matter of managing by taking informed risks within clearly defined boundaries of acceptability. The trouble is that these boundaries, which are supposed to be fixed and secure, have a tendency to get moved, not by design but by acquiescence. This is especially the case when the going is good.

Thus, people are likely to inform you, as the leader of your organization, of those things that they think you would prefer to hear or to present them to you in ways that they believe will be most likely to be acceptable or pleasing to you. Truth often hurts and the organization is rare indeed that encourages people to hurt its bosses. We all have a tendency to shy away from those situations that we find embarrassing or threatening and many of us are inclined to project this tendency onto others, particularly when those others have power and authority over us. So it is quite likely that your managers will take it upon themselves, to protect you from information that they would find personally embarrassing or threatening were they to find themselves in your position. Moreover, some people in leadership positions unwittingly (or knowingly) encourage such behavior. Thus, the exhortation to, "bring me solutions, not problems", can easily degenerate, in fact if not by intention, into, "don't bring me bad news."

At the workshop described earlier in this chapter, Professor Argyris suggested that organizational behavior was influenced strongly by two kinds of theories that are often in conflict:

"Espoused theories" are those that are concerned with what the organization's leaders would like to be true about it. "Theories in use", on the other hand concern the ways in which people within the organization perceive that things get done in practice. While the former tend to be written down and formally communicated, the latter tend to be communicated verbally and informally, over coffee, or in the pub through stories, jokes and anecdotes. These theories in use are widely shared but are very rarely openly acknowledged and certainly not upwards and between levels in the organizational hierarchy.

Here are a couple of examples of theories in use from Graham's research.

2.3.1   How to appoint directors

Asked how appointments were made to his public company's board of directors, the HR director of a major manufacturing company stated that there was an appointments committee that made a selection between candidates against a number of written criteria. *"However, only those who have been to Oxford, rather than Cambridge, have served in the Army and who could hold their own at a Buckingham Palace garden party would ever be considered. This is, of course, why HR is not represented on the main board."* This was not simply a matter of sour grapes. Checking out the bio-graphies of the company's board members suggested that every one would have met these criteria for selection.

2.3.2 Watching for his lips to move

In another company one director in particular appeared to suffer from a lack of trust on the part of his colleagues. One of them was asked why he thought this might be, "*Well*", came the reply, "*When you see his lips move, you can be pretty sure that he is lying.*" It became apparent that this cruel joke was circulating widely in the company. Whether or not it had any justification is beside the point. The fact that it was in circulation had a negative impact on both the director's and the board's effectiveness.

We think that it is critically important for you, as leader of the organization, to strive through the example of your own behavior to minimize the difference between Argyris' two kinds of theory – theories espoused and theories in use. This requires you to be clearly aware of the values to which you adhere and upon which you will never, ever be prepared to compromise. If these values aren't clear to you now, when they come to be tested by the unexpected opportunities or crises that arise, you may find that they have already been compromised in ways from which recovery is extremely difficult, if not impossible. Moreover, if they are not clear to you, how can they be clear to those whom you lead?

The captain of a lifeboat, a fire chief or pilot of a supersonic fighter aircraft tend to be pretty clear about such things. For them to fudge them would be to put their own lives and those of their colleagues and the many others who depend upon them at risk. But is it any different if you find yourself at the head of an oil exploration company and learn at the end of quarter one that the company's reserves are not quite as you thought they were, nor as you had stated them to be at the end of the previous financial year? You have a business to run and the company's share price is critical. Perhaps you might convince yourself that the chances are that, if your highly talented and experienced exploration geologists and petroleum engineers pull out all the stops, it is very likely that the shortfall will be made up before the figures need to be republished. You might well be right and, besides, isn't business all about judgment and risk-taking anyway?

But where do you draw the line? Our view is that if you only get round to drawing the line at the moment when such issues arise, it is quite likely that it has already been moved a long way from where you believe it should be. It won't necessarily have been shifted by you, but by others in the organization, who thought that they were "protecting your interests", long before you came around to ensuring that such interests were unequivocally defined and universally understood. But now it is too late. If you find as leader of your organization that you are on this slippery slope, you can be pretty sure that others are already well on their way toward reaching its bottom.

In the worlds of volatile commodity prices and frenetic city dealing rooms, no one's life is likely to be lost as a direct consequence of an ill-judged action or decision. However, millions may be wiped off your company's share price and careers may be destroyed as a result of a misplaced decimal point that has been unwittingly or deliberately concealed. Your judgment may well be right and the figures may come good by the year-end, but if you permit or acquiesce in the suppression or concealment of inaccurate information, your integrity and that of your organization has been seriously compromised. The message that your action will have conveyed within the organization is likely to have done much more damage than would have been the consequence of sharing the knowledge of the shortfall and taking steps to correct it.

So when we talk about managing the unexpected, we are talking about the nature of your response, the message that it conveys and what it tells the world about you, as much as we are talking about dealing with unexpected events themselves. Our concern is with the manner in which you seize the moment when it arrives, regardless of whether it offers you a magnificent opportunity, presents you with a crisis of epic proportions or involves you in missing your ten year old daughter's school play. Such messages are about you, your values, your standards and your personal integrity and they are extremely important.

Leading is as much about knowing, remembering and being who you are as it is about what you do. It is about making sure that what you say you do and what you do in practice are as close to being congruent as you can possibly make them. Far too many top managers publish their organizations' "values", hang them on the walls where everybody can see them and then act in ways that run contrary to them every day of every week. There is nothing wrong in publishing your aspirations, provided that you are ready and willing to have it pointed out to you when you fail to live up to them. But please don't confuse your aspirations with your values. We all slip up every now and then but very few of us are prepared to compromise our genuine values (or our prejudices, to look at the issue from another angle), while we probably feel a lot less uncomfortable when we fail to meet an aspiration. After all, there's always tomorrow.

2.4 The call center project

John knows of a company that introduced an experimental call center in one of its divisions when such centers were in their infancy and when the level of integration of the i.t. and communications technology that such centers employ today was relatively underdeveloped. The concept was piloted in one of the company's sales regions as a means of testing and developing the company's approach to customer care. However, the pilot project revealed a significant problem that the CEO and his managers had not realized existed. While management had been focusing its attention on the speed of response, courtesy and levels of caller satisfaction, the call center technology revealed the fact that a high proportion of callers were never receiving *any* kind of response from the company at all. This was because the telephone was either engaged; remained unanswered or held the caller suspended in a queue for so long that he or she rang off without having spoken to anybody. No one in the company seemed to have been aware that this was happening, never mind knowing just how

big the problem was. Prior to the pilot, they had not possessed nor thought of acquiring any means of knowing,
let alone measuring, the scale of the problem. Its identifica-
tion was an unexpected and quite unintended consequence
of the pilot study and caused the CEO to totally revise
the way that he and his company understood their ideas
about customer care and to conduct a fundamental review
of the nature of the company's communication with its
customers.

Prior to this revelation, the company had viewed itself as
being a sophisticated player in its own, particular market,
confident of its ability to move its products around the
country in response to customer demand. However, though
the company's profitability levels were acceptable and
despite being well ahead of the competition, its senior
management had recognized that it was beginning to lose
market share, hence its renewed interest in customer care.
The discovery at the regional call center pilot revealed
that the company was on the edge of a black hole without
anyone ever having realized it. Many potential, existing
and soon-to-be ex-customers were trying to communicate
with the company and failing in the attempt. It wasn't
that no one had ever talked about the issue previously,
no one had even *thought* about it before. Once identified,
however, the problem opened up many new opportunities
for the company because it revealed just how the instal-
lation of a new technology could enable it to benchmark
itself against businesses completely outside its market but
for which excellent company communications were a sine
qua non.

The CEO recalled, "*When it comes to service, customers
don't just wonder if they'll get better service from the next
widget supplier; they ask themselves why, if they can receive
excellent service from their travel agent, their online bank, or
their garage, are they not getting it from us? We were in competition for customer service quality just as much as we were
in competition for the volumes of product that we sold*".

The trigger of an unexpected event (in this example it was the revelation of a company-wide problem through a local pilot project) took the company's management out of its comfort zone and eventually resulted in a transformation of its attitudes, organization structures and even its location; it also resulted in radically improved profitability levels.

2.6 Be on the lookout for signals

Such transformations often require the trigger of an unexpected event that causes an organization to break out of the constraints of habit, assumptions and inertia that constantly silt up its ability to flex, to adapt and to reconfigure itself in the light of new circumstances.

Do such triggers always need to involve a crisis?

Our guess is that, in the end, it is likely to come down to the willingness of the person at the top to make a point of listening out for signals that might be the harbingers of an unexpected event or a change, whether in the form of a potential crisis or of an opportunity. Such signals may be being picked up lower down the organization (as was shown to have been the case in the two, NASA space shuttle disasters) but are being screened out at those lower levels by a number of all too familiar devices:

"It's not my problem/responsibility";

"I assumed that you would know about that";

"I thought that it might be a good idea, but no-one has ever asked me for my opinion, so I never thought to mention it."

So:

2.6.1 Listen out for signals - especially weak ones

What we are talking about here is the way in which an organization's collective mindset informs the view of everyone in it about the way things are and how they ought to be. Such mindsets permeate every aspect of an organization's life and may be positive or negative. They can challenge or stretch or drag down and depress. They are also reflections of aspects of an organization's leadership style.

We don't wish to give the impression that we believe that the organizational leader should act like some kind of high-level inspector, walking about the organization looking for unsecured ladders, with a finger ready to wag in disapproval, until the guilty are hunted down and punished. It isn't a matter of catching people out. In our experience such a management style only encourages people to hide their mistakes rather than to avoid making them in the first place – to cover up rather than to correct.

Your job as organizational leader is to work diligently in order to develop a mindset within the organization where people act instinctively to avoid error. When they do make a mistake, or when they identify an error made by someone else, their reaction should be to make sure that the error is corrected. This requires an organizational climate in which blame is not the name of the game. But only the person at the top can ensure that this is the case, by behaving in ways that put the need for corrective action to be regarded as being far more important than the desire to blame, punish or to hide errors.

Since, "if you've never made a mistake, you have probably never done anything that was worth doing."

Every one of us makes mistakes and the organization's mindset needs to acknowledge this in order to encourage responses that show that it is everyone's responsibility to ensure that, once identified, no unsecured ladder remains that way for very long.

Therefore, getting to a state in which such a mindset is the norm rather than the exception is a key responsibility of the person at the top of the organization. Developing and setting a positive organizational mindset is a challenge, but one that is not only worth taking on, it is a challenge that no organizational leader can avoid. Those at the top manage by example – so they should do their best to ensure that the example that they offer is a good one.

This raises a paradox. We are arguing that there are some things in an organization that should never be questioned, challenged or compromised – the preeminence over everything of people's safety, for example. Here the company mindset should be that we never deviate from the path of safety because, if we do, the well-being of customers, employees, the public at large and we ourselves will be at risk.

On the other hand it is equally axiomatic that, if you as leader want your organization to thrive and to grow, then people need to be encouraged to question, to explore and to challenge in the interests of creativity and innovation. The person who must take on the act of juggling these paradoxical elements of conformity and challenge is the person at the top and that is ... you.

2.7   Summarizing so far ...

People at the top of organizations have to deal with unexpected events. These are inevitable, whether they are genuine events, being of the kind that arise within the organization's wider environment and where the specific event could not have been anticipated, or whether they are the cumulative consequence of errors that could and should have been identified and corrected but which were not.

Either way, the impact of such events is similar in that they demand an immediate response and are a major test of the person at the top's abilities as a leader.

A challenge to you as a leader is to work to ensure that there is sufficient flexibility and "slack" within the system to enable the organization to respond to unexpected events of the genuine kind so that their potential negative consequences are as much as possible kept under your control. But it is equally important for you to encourage a climate that, while not punitive nor blame driven, shows zero tolerance for the conditions that give rise to unexpected events which are the results of consequential error.

It takes time and effort to bring about such a change in an organization's climate, particularly, as in cases like the organizations of those of us who attended Professor Argyris' workshop where "chronic errors" had been allowed to be committed for a very long time. But the costs of not challenging such a negative climate are far greater in the long run, when events occur that should never have been allowed to happen in the first place.

This requires you to have the courage to confront and then to break bad organizational habits that may be of many years standing. In doing so you will encounter both open and tacit opposition. Therefore, taking on the challenge of being the leader of your organization also requires you to be prepared to remove from the organization those who are doing it damage. This does not mean that you have to be ruthless but it does mean that you have to be tough and be ready to engage in some difficult conversations – not least with yourself. These conversations are likely to include ones with senior colleagues who have served the organization well, but who have tolerated what you as leader should not tolerate. You cannot afford to let such discrepancies rest.

2.8 An obstacle course

Before we conclude this chapter we want to consider some of the obstacles that can limit your ability to manage unexpected events effectively when they occur.

2.7.1 Make time and space for reflection and review

One such obstacle arises as a consequence of permitting outmoded or outdated policies, processes and procedures to remain in use long beyond their usefulness. These three "Ps" need to be subjected to continuous critical review and, possibly, reengineered. Too often they are detached from the priorities of the business, having been delegated to specialist staff functions whose members may not wish, be able or be allowed to get to grips with matters that are of crucial importance to it. Thus, for example, we encounter senior HR professionals who don't see it as being their role or place to offer a view on the return on the investment on the human capital employed within the business. We meet others who would not know where to begin to interpret a balance sheet. But these same people can turn out an excellent policy on equal opportunities or dignity at work. Please don't misunderstand us; we are not for one moment saying that such policies are unimportant. But we do say that they need to make sense in the context of the organization's core business priorities, to the people who are accountable for delivering against these priorities and within the wider context within which the business operates. If those who draft such policies have little appreciation of this context and are not expected to be fully engaged with it, they cannot be blamed if the policies that they generate do not fit. That accountability lies higher up the organization. It rests with you.

In the words of Jim Collins in his book, Good to Great, "you need to get the right people on the bus."[6] These are people who understand what it is that you wish to achieve and share with you a passion for achieving it.

2.7.2 Watch out for hubris!

A second obstacle to coping effectively with the unexpected is hubris.

The word "hubris" comes from the Greek, "hybris", which roughly translates as, excessive pride or belief in one's own capabilities and importance to the point of self-destruction. It carries with it the suggestion of presumptuousness, the pride that comes before a fall and the inevitability of eventual disaster. Lest you think that we are becoming overly negative once again, the prophets of doom that we didn't set out to be, we see hubris as being more a problem of success rather than of failure. It is quite likely that as many businesses are killed off by hubris, born of their leaders' past successes and their overweening sense of self-belief, as are brought down by any particular strengths on the part of their competitors or by the arrival of difficult market conditions.

In a recent article in the neurological journal 'Brain'[7], Lord David Owen and Jonathan Davidson suggest that hubris might be regarded as a medical condition (an acquired personality disorder) that is as much an occupational hazard for those in positions of power and leadership as repetitive strain injury is for people who work all day at a keyboard. They suggest that there are a number of symptoms for what they label 'hubris syndrome' including those that we have derived from their list of fourteen and have listed below. Ask yourself how many of these symptoms you might be displaying – better still, ask your spouse or partner.

2.5   Symptoms of hubris?

- A tendency to see the world primarily as an arena in which you can exercise power and look for personal glory
- An excessive concern with your image and the way in which you present yourself to the world
- A concern to pursue and focus your attention upon actions that are likely to show you in a good light
- Developing a style of speech that tends towards the messianic and a tendency to exaggeration and exaltation
- Excessive confidence in your own judgements together with a tendency to disregard the opinions, advice and criticism of other people
- An exaggerated belief in yourself and your abilities that could be seen as bordering on a sense of omnipotence
- Increasing incompetence in addressing things that go wrong within the organisation because of a loss of interest in and contact with detail and the nuts and bolts of policy, arising from excessive confidence in yourself and a tendency to have less and less confidence in others.

Owen and Davidson suggest that people who display more than three or four such symptoms could well be on the way to developing hubris syndrome and a fully fledged personality disorder. They go on to argue that several recent US Presidents and UK Prime Ministers had quite clearly done just this. They propose that antidotes to the poisonous effects and often tragic consequences of these symptoms might be found by ensuring that you develop a sense of collective or shared accountability with your colleagues at the top together with a willingness to question and sometimes challenge one another including you as their leader. They also recommend having access to an independent and respected mentor; someone who is not afraid to hold up the mirror to your behavior without flinching, encouraging you to see yourself as others see you – warts and all. We would add the benefits of a strong team of non-executive directors, willing to ask you the questions that you would rather they didn't and of having strong and honest relationships in your personal life.

We argued earlier that encouraging a mindset within which making mistakes is recognized as being inevitable is very difficult but necessary. In our view, the mindset that is needed can only be generated via high quality leadership. But, as an organization's leader you are in no way immune from making errors. The paradox here is to be able to demonstrate your fallibility without in any way undermining the authority of your leadership role.

How many government ministers will raise their hands and admit that they have got it wrong? Did the men at the helms of Lehman Brothers (Dick Fuld) and of Northern Rock (Adam Applegarth) admit to their questioners from Congress or the House of Commons that it was their actions and decisions that had led to the collapse of the banks that they led? No they didn't. Both stuck fast to the view that they could have done absolutely nothing differently from what they had done. Even though one of them accepted that he had been trying to effect a sale of the bank at a price that would leave his pride intact immediately before the collapse, while the other maintained that no one could have foreseen what had happened, notwithstanding the fact that the committee that was questioning him had been discussing it for the previous six weeks.

Why is it, even when their reputations are already shot to pieces, that people continue to deny the consequences of their actions? Because they hold sets of totally incompatible or dissonant beliefs, that is, two or more beliefs that are mutually incompatible.

Thus I may believe myself to be a highly competent chief executive, while at the same time I am confronted by the fact that the bank that I lead has just gone bust. I resolve the incompatibility by finding or generating new "facts" that I believe will reconcile it, at least to my own satisfaction. Thus I claim that the bank's collapse was caused not by any action of mine but by global recession; the UK government is similarly the victim of unpredictable global forces; the child died because someone (else) failed to follow the correct procedures; the war was lost because we were betrayed, etc.

I am basically a good guy, the fact that it may appear that I have done something very wrong can be explained by:

- blaming somebody else;
- explaining that what appears to have been an incorrect action did not, in fact, take place;
- Saying that what I did was permissible within the rules;
- convincing myself that I was somewhere else at the time;
- a plea of temporary insanity.

The greater the error, the more difficult it seems to be to acknowledge it. This is presumably why only a limited number of murderers call the police to let them know what they have done.

We strongly advocate that every leader needs a mentor, someone who has the leader's respect and trust; who is knowledgeable in the arena within which the leader is operating and who has no personal stake in the leader's business. Someone who has both the personal courage and the integrity to shine the light on every aspect of the leader's activity, holding them up to the mirror without flinching and without judging for, unless the leader is capable of exercising such judgment him or herself, the mentor no matter how wise is likely to be reduced to the ranks of someone else who does not understand or who can be blamed.

Developing hubris when at the top prevents you from anticipating the unexpected. So we see it as being a very important word to bear in mind when endeavoring to shape the future – one that every leader should constantly recall to remind them of its dangers and as an encouragement to reflect and consider if perhaps they are approaching the point of no return.

Self-insight, self-awareness and self-understanding are essential leadership qualities in the battle to stop self-belief degenerating into hubris. These qualities require space for self-reflection to help you ensure that you remain in touch with your values. We are not advocating long periods of navel gazing and self-criticism. But we do think that if you are to be truly effective as a leader over the long term, then you need to be able to stand back and reflect. This is a great deal easier with the help of a mentor to hold up the mirror to what you are doing and are becoming, without judgment but without flinching.

2.9 Some more questions

In conclusion, we believe that the risk of those unexpected events of the type that we have described as "genuine" being allowed to decay and to generate "cumulative consequential errors" is most likely to occur in organizations that have a track record of success but where rules are regularly broken, where policies and procedures are inconsistent, inappropriately located, or developed out of context and where processes are not subjected to regular review. In such organizations leaders are likely to find themselves increasingly in the business of defense, self-justification and recovery of reputation rather than of innovation, creativity and development.

So:

- How often and how much time do you spend quietly reflecting and planning the future?
- What was the last mistake that you made?
- To whom did you admit that mistake?
- Do you have someone that you trust and who you permit to give you honest and objective feedback about what and how you are doing? Do you/would you listen, really listen to such a person even when what you were hearing was hurtful to you?
- How do you react when colleagues bring you good news and/or report good performance? Do you publicly celebrate, acknowledging their success? Do you consider giving them a bonus? Do you thank them and ask them to keep up the good work? Do you recognize that is what you pay them to do? Does your position inhibit you from showing too much enthusiasm?
- How do you react when colleagues bring you bad news and/ or poor performance? Do you blow your top? Do you ask to know whose fault it was? Do you ask what is being done to put it right? Do you ask how you could help to put things right?
- Typically, how does your organization react when mistakes are made? Are you sure about this? Do you really know?

- How many innovative experiments, pilot projects or trials are currently in progress within your organization? How often do you seek to find out how they are doing?
- How aware are you of any unofficial, "pirate" or "rogue" experiments, projects and trials that may be going on in your organization? How do (or would) you feel about them? What action would you take if and when they became "public" knowledge?
- What is your organization's official attitude toward such unofficial, "pirate" or "rogue" experiments, projects or trials that may be being undertaken with the company's materials and on its time?
- What kinds of future, contingency or scenario planning are carried out in your organization? How often are they reviewed? Who is involved and with whom are their findings shared?
- How would you describe the culture of your organization to a friend who does not know it well? How well do you think it reflects your own values and principles? How do you feel about it? What would you like to change and how might you go about it?
- In the past, how have you responded to unexpected events that are:
  - A: Genuine – that is, that have arisen from circumstances in the wider environment that are outside your or your organization's control?
  - B: Cumulative consequence – that is, a consequence of errors that have previously occurred within the organization?
- When answering the previous question, how did you determine the difference between events of type A and type B?
- What do your answers to these questions suggest to you about the way in which you are leading your organization?

CHAPTER 3

Attitudes and the unexpected

3.1 Setting the tone

In the previous chapter we stated that the ways in which organizations respond to unexpected events is largely determined by its prevalent mindset. An organization's prevailing mindset, in turn, is shaped by the values, attitudes and behaviors of its leaders and reflected in the way it deals with mistakes. For example, it may result in their being perceived as a fact of life for which allowances must be made or as failures, the perpetrators of which need to be discovered, humiliated and punished. It may encourage errors to be hidden, denied and covered up. It may mean that blame is the name of the game or encourage people to freely acknowledge when they have made a mistake so that both they and the organization may learn from them. Whatever complexion an organization's mindset may develop, its tone is significantly influenced by its leadership.

In this chapter we explore some of the ways in which the attitudes that leaders hold come to set the tone, climate and mindset of their organization; how these attitudes are revealed in the ways that leaders respond to unexpected events and how they shape the responses of the people that they lead. We consider how these combine in providing the stories and myths that shape the character of the organization. We conclude by asking some more questions, the answers to which may help to bring your own, underlying attitudes and values to the surface.

We believe that one of the obligations that falls to the leader of an organization is to take responsibility for setting and managing its tone. Presumably, this is what boards of directors intend when they commission consultants to help them to articulate their strategic intentions, business plans and statements of corporate values. But this is only part of the story.

Unless your personal values, your actions and your behaviors are seen to be congruent with those strategies, goals and values, the effort and money expended in their articulation and publication is likely to prove to have been a distraction and, therefore, a waste of time. Leadership cannot be delegated. Experts are no substitute for leadership, though, as we shall see, their support is essential to the successful management of the unexpected.

Setting the tone of the organization isn't something that you can take for granted. In your leadership role you are going to do it anyway, since every action you take and every statement or decision you make reflects your values, your attitudes and your beliefs. So you need to be mindful of the tone that you are setting – that is to be fully aware of the impact that your behavior has upon others and how different groups of people are likely to interpret it and respond to it – both on and off the job.

Whatever a leader does provides a model, an example to the organization as a whole, to its stakeholders and to the market within which it operates. Unless you are aware of the nature of the example that you are setting, you risk conveying one that is inconsistent with the goals that you wish the organization to pursue and the values that you wish its members to hold. Such inconsistencies rarely go unnoticed. We put our credibility at risk when we convince ourselves that they do not matter, because we are conveying the message that people should do as we say, not as we do. We are then under pressure to modify the perceptions that people have of events in the interests of preserving our image. As Pierre Corneille wrote many years ago, "a good memory is needed once we have lied." The risk to our personal credibility is significantly increased if, when the unexpected occurs (as it will), it takes us by surprise. It is then that we are most likely to let the genie out of the bottle and reveal those parts of ourselves that we would rather have remained hidden.

We can all think of leaders who clearly set the tone and character of the businesses that they run, for good or ill. Over the past 20 years or so, their stories have been told many times in the media, while their biographies are displayed in airport bookstalls the world over. They have become celebrities and as such their stories, their lifestyles and their peccadilloes are as regularly analysed and publicly displayed as are their business successes and failures – Richard Branson, Robert Maxwell, Bill Gates, Lord Browne, Sir Alan Sugar, Steve Jobs, Jack Welch to name just a few. But we are not arguing that setting the tone of the organization is something that is just an option for the business leader who wishes to get onto the celebrity circuit. It is, as we have said, an obligation that goes with the role. The only choice that organizational leaders get to exercise in the matter concerns the quality of the tone that they set through the messages conveyed by their attitudes and behaviors and the extent to which they are prepared to make themselves aware of the myths and stories that are told about them.

3.2   Awareness, reflection and the management of expectations

3.2.1   "The unexamined life is a life not worth living."[1]

To exercise choice in this area requires a high degree of self-insight and self-awareness that is unlikely to be present without your being willing to step back and consciously reflect upon who you are and how you come to be as and where you are.

Where did the attitudes and values that you hold come from? How do they come to shape your behavior and how do they go on to shape the tone of your organization?

Each of us brings a lifetime's baggage of attitudes, prejudices and assumptions to the work roles that we play, whether we are a school-leaver, newly appointed to her first full-time job, an "old sweat" in the back office, a divisional director or a chief executive of a multinational corporation. Each of us has a history, much of it helpful and some of it less so, and we bring it with us to work every day.

Our attitudes are shaped by our past; by the ways in which were brought up, by the ways in which we were educated and trained, by the experiences that we have had and by all that we have learned from them. There is a significant obstacle to our becoming mindful of our underlying attitudes, however, in that the roots in which they are so firmly anchored are, as is the way with roots, largely below the surface. As such they tend not to feature at a high level in our consciousness or of our awareness. They are simply "there" where we can easily take them for granted, becoming unaware of their existence. This can get us into difficulties.

There appears to be a consensus among psychologists, psychiatrists, biologists and neuroscientists that a great many of the choices that we make and upon which we base our decisions are made at a level that also lies deep beneath that of which we are conscious or aware. Some people might describe the decision choices made in this way as being intuitive, or as being based on experience, nous, or as having been made through the application of tacit knowledge (knowledge that we seem to possess without knowing where it has come from and which we are unable to put into words).

It doesn't matter just how decisions at this, "undermind"[2] level come to be made. The point is that we are likely to be unaware of the fact that we have made a particular choice after we have already excluded a number of other equally possible choices at a level of which we are not conscious. Our brains make these initial choices on the basis of a rapid sifting of our previous experiences, rather than on a self-conscious analysis of what needs to be done, right here and right now.

3.1   Tackling the right problem?

Some years ago Graham conducted an assessment centre that was designed to help the directors of a company that owned a national chain of betting shops to select a senior regional manager. The candidates were asked to analyse a fictitious consultant's report of the pros and cons associated with the possible acquisition of a much smaller, family-owned group of betting shops. One candidate was clearly delighted with this particular task and rapidly came to a conclusion with which he expressed himself to be totally satisfied. He left the assessment centre fully confident that the job was his.

Later, when asked why he had been so confident, the candidate explained that he had been involved in just such a case a few months earlier and that, as a result, he "knew" the answer. The assessors, however, reported that while he had provided a very interesting example of the *kind of situation* that was involved in the task, he had missed several issues that were critical to the particular case in point. He had, in effect, come up with a good solution to what was actually quite a different problem.

We register that something has happened. Our brains process the information they have received about that "something", rapidly categorize it, and compare it with other events within that category that are already stored in our memory. In this way, we make sense of an event in terms of its similarity to other events that we have experienced in the past. The process is already well under way by the time we become conscious of the fact that something has happened and that we need to respond to it. So several options for possible solutions have been excluded before we know that we have a problem!

So the brain, miraculous as it is, doesn't always get it right. We tend to see what we expect to see, emphasizing those things that confirm our expectations and suppressing those things that do not. In this way, what we find in life is often the product of what it was that we were looking for, rather than that for which we needed to be on the look out.

At the level of consciousness we carry a range of further expectations including, for example, the expectation that what has worked well in the past is likely to work well in the future. This expectation is valuable in conditions characterized by routine and stability because it helps to limit the number and range of things that we have to think about and upon which we need to focus our attention. But it may also cause us to miss the symptoms and signals that presage the occurrence of an unexpected event, thereby reducing our capacity to deal with it appropriately when it happens.

This can also happen more formally. The plans that we make tend to emphasize our expectations and, as a result, limit the range of things that we notice, suppressing or excluding things that are outside the range of our expectations. Thus our plans may actually work to increase the number of potential sources of the unexpected events that may undermine them. The plans that we develop for the future are worked out in the present and are likely to assume that the things that have worked well in the past and are working well right now will continue to do so in future. Therefore, they tend to limit the range of our expectations of the unusual and the unexpected.

We are inclined to notice those things that confirm our expectations and give us the comfort of feeling that we are on the right track. But, as a leader, unless you make a conscious effort to look out for the unusual, the discrepant and the erroneous; unless, while striving for success you are also constantly on the look out for symptoms of failure, you are unlikely to notice the symptoms of the unexpected when they first confront you. Worse still, when demonstrated in a leadership role, such behavior is likely to discourage other people from looking out for such symptoms of the unusual and the unexpected as well. It is a great deal easier to tell the boss what she would like to hear than it is to tell her that which she would rather not know.

> During routine operations members of typical organizations demonstrate deference to the powerful, the coercive, the senior and the experienced, forgetting that they may have had the same experience over and over, were never on the shop floor, are unfamiliar with the industry, were not around when the plan was constructed or got their position through politics.[3]

People in such positions are likely to get nothing but filtered good news.

You need to be sure that you are fully aware of your predispositions and to subject them to regular critical examination. If you don't, you may well fall into the trap of taking decisions that owe more to your assumptions and to your habits than they do to sound evidence and a thorough analysis of what the situation may demand.

Put it another way: if you are to reduce the risk that your reaction to an unexpected event owes more to an experience that you had last year, in a previous job or even in your childhood, then you are going to need the self-insight that will enable you to recognize this possibility and build it into your strategic approach.

Many psychometric questionnaires and other tools are available to directors and managers that can help you to identify your "psychological type", your "leadership style" or your "work preferences" and enable you to share that identity with others should you so choose.[4] They can be very helpful as a means to assist you in developing your understanding of the different ways in which you are likely to interact with colleagues and staff with mental sets and constructs that differ from your own and of the ways in which you are likely to respond to the unexpected when it happens. The research upon which such instruments are based tends to support our contention that the extent to which we are surprised by an unexpected event and, therefore, the manner in which we respond to it, is largely predetermined by our past experiences. These, in their turn, have shaped the attitudes and values that we hold.

3.3   Challenge your expectations

In circumstances of risk, instability and high uncertainty, our expectations need to be counterbalanced by a dose of healthy skepticism and doubt. It doesn't matter whether this counterbalance is formalized in policies, statements of strategic intent, business plans or corporate values, or whether it is communicated informally, for example, through the things that we are seen to smile upon and those which are assumed to be likely to upset or offend us; the kinds of people that we reward and those that we don't. We need to ensure that we subject such expectations to constant questioning and challenge if we are not to fall into the trap of leading the organization by means of a mental automatic pilot that is governed by our habits and our expectations.

You can provide such a counterbalance by being self-consciously on the look out for symptoms and signals that might indicate that things could be happening that are inconsistent with your expectations – and then to encourage everyone else in the organization to do the same. As your organization's leader, you cannot afford to permit such signals to be missed – no matter how weak and trivial they may appear to be.

Unless we regularly step back to reflect and deliberately bring some of our underlying attitudes to the forefront of our consciousness where they can be tested and opened up to being challenged, we are likely to forget or be unaware that we hold them, let alone to be aware of the degree to which they influence our decision-making and determine our actions.

Such reflection starts at a very basic level.

For example, do you, on balance, tend to see your life as being half full or half empty? Does your perception of the world shift from day to day, depending on circumstances? How do you react to people of other generations, other races, and other sexual orientation? Are you a different person at home and in your personal life from the person who you are when at work? If so, why might this be?

We are not looking for you to provide the "right" answer to such questions, we suggest only that you are aware of what your answers would be, why that might be so and how your answers stack up against the values and attitudes that you claim to espouse.

Events that are unexpected have the effect of changing the rules of the game in ways that can be quite unnerving. Very often the unexpected event doesn't seem to fit the context in which it occurs. The explosion of a terrorist's bomb on a commuter train is an extreme example. But so too is the sudden exposure of a trusted advisor who has been feeding you duff information, the person who looks like a tramp but speaks to you in a refined accent and turns out to hold a significant number of your company's shares, or the impact of the collapse of a currency and the windfall profits or losses that this may bring to your business.

Such things tend to make a great deal more sense in retrospect than they do at the time that they occur. When something happens completely out of the blue and which does not fit comfortably with the context in which it has occurred, we may be initially and literally dumbfounded, behaving in ways that seem totally out of character and inexplicable – both to ourselves and to others.

A few years ago, for example, Graham had a skiing accident in which he dislocated his shoulder. For the half hour or so following the accident, he was totally convinced that his shoulder would soon "get better" even though he was unable to raise his arm above the level of his waist. Desperate to continue to enjoy his holiday (which had only just begun), he was in complete denial of what the evidence was telling him. The brain starts to search for a reference point, for something that matches what has just occurred to one's expectations, in order to "know" how to respond. As in this example, it can get it wrong!

3.2   Business as usual?

As the shares of the British bank Northern Rock went into free fall in early 2008 and depositors started queuing around the block to withdraw their savings, one of its directors commented to a television interviewer that while "business was as usual", the future was going to involve a great deal of hard work in order to "rebuild the brand." We wonder how that comment went down with customers who feared that they were about to lose their savings, and with mortgage holders who saw themselves threatened with the repossession of their homes. "Rebuilding the brand" may have been intended to address their concerns. But if it was, it was said in the wrong language, appearing to be more concerned with the security of the Bank than that of the customers on whom its survival depended. Business was very far from being "as usual" no matter how much the director might have wished it to be.

Our post-event sense-making processes can cause us to reinterpret what has happened in ways that we hope will protect our self-esteem and our self-interests rather than helping us to address a problem requiring our focused attention toward finding an urgent resolution. So, just as it is wise to ensure that you avoid making an instant response to an unexpected incident on the basis of the shock to your system that it represents, you also need to move swiftly to investigate the factors that have lead to its occurrence. Is it "genuine" or an event that is a "cumulative consequence" of things that you should have known about and dealt with much earlier? Failing to do this quickly puts you at risk of being misled by the information with which you are provided about the event that is, in any case, likely to have been modified in order to protect backsides, self-esteem and egos.

You need to ensure that one of those backsides is not your own.

3.4   Some risks of categorization

In Graham's recent study of directors who were charged with driving major changes through their organizations, he noted a tendency among most of them to describe their changes as though each was a discrete project. These directors were likely to see such projects as being quite distinct from their other responsibilities and, in particular, as separate from those concerning routine operational matters. Some of them labeled such responsibilities, "business as usual", and felt that they could be safely delegated to others, while they concentrated their energies on leading their change "projects".

The "language" that the directors used to describe these change projects tended to be somewhat formal, incorporating the rational, analytical terminology of project management and business planning techniques and a good deal of "business speak". Their projects were presented as being logical, with planned beginning and end dates, and programmed to deliver against a planned set of objectives and milestones. But, "when people are in thrall to [the] predetermination [of plans], there is simply no place for unexpected events that fall outside the realm of planning."[5] Some of the directors, though by no means all of them, identified very strongly with their project, seeing it as being a personal responsibility; something that was strictly "down to them" and which they "owned." The attention of these directors tended to be focused inwards upon their ownership, their sense of responsibility, their personal contribution and upon the isolation of their senior position.

A few of the directors in this group combined this inward personal focus with a perspective toward the wider context in which their change project was located that was confined to areas that were for the most part within the boundaries of their organization. Thus, they would describe "their" project in terms of the organizational structural and process issues that were involved in bringing about the changes that they wished to see. They were much less likely to discuss it in terms that showed it to be a response to bigger changes that were taking place in the wider business environment.

When unexpected events occurred in that wider environment, this last group of directors was very likely to be caught off-balance and to be taken by surprise. Its members tended to be hit particularly hard by the consequences of such events and to experience more difficulty in responding to them swiftly. They were less likely to deliver an appropriate response than were those directors who displayed a more outwardly directed personal focus (e.g. one that engaged their colleagues, the teams involved in making the changes and that took account of their likely implications for people who were not directly involved in making them a success) and a broader, and externally oriented contextual perspective (e.g. toward the wider social, economic and political environment in which their businesses were operating).

When they described the impact of such events, the "language" used by these directors was far from the rational, analytic style of project management that they had used when they had initially described their change projects. It was more personal, much more emotionally raw, and was clearly more deeply felt.

The following quotations from interview transcripts illustrate what we mean:

3.3 A CEO's experience of a takeover bid by a major shareholder

"I never in a million years thought they would do that … and I behaved as though I thought they would never do it. Now, had someone taken me aside or had I sat down and thought, 'this is an assumption that you're not entitled to make— they might just do it', things might have been different. When they did, it was like a physical hammer blow. I couldn't speak. I couldn't believe what had happened and was in shock."

Making sense of a boardroom battle after the event

"I have been far too trusting in my life. I believed that people behaved for the good of the company. I would suggest to you that seventy five per cent of them don't. Either because of ambition or because of insecurity, the two often go together. You cannot trust people. Be very careful."

In both these cases the directors involved indicated that the events that had taken them by surprise had probably been instigated by a cunning and unscrupulous shareholder or by villains within their companies. But the events concerned had in fact both been triggered by changes that had nothing to do with their companies and that were totally beyond their companies' control. These were events that took place within a much wider environment than the local one within which the directors and their projects were immersed. Some of their colleagues' responses may indeed have been villainous, but the directors had failed to anticipate them as a consequence, at least in part, of their inappropriately narrow, inward focus and a lack of preparation and anticipation when the events occurred and, so, they were taken by surprise.

Their reactions were understandable but inappropriate.

By then it was too late. Their reactions were primarily directed toward dealing with the responses of others within the organization's boundaries rather than toward dealing with and containing the consequences of the events themselves, appreciating their external origins and addressing the problems that they represented.

3.5 Good leadership or good luck?

The above examples clearly relate to bad experiences for the directors involved but they might well have responded just as inappropriately to positive events and have missed the opportunities that such events can offer. Thus the unexpected event that generates a windfall profit to your business needs to be recognized for the good luck that it is rather than as one that provides evidence of your leadership brilliance.

As John observes:

> I have been in boardrooms where I have been appalled by the way in which what was clearly a lucky break has been represented as being the consequence of the successful outcome of some wickedly cunning and ingenious plan. I am not in any way averse to taking advantage of and giving thanks for good luck when it happens. But I do not see why we should kid ourselves that we should take or give any credit for it. I suppose it was my technical training that gave me the discipline to insist that decision-making should always be based on evidence, on measurement and that the decision should be shown to lie within the boundaries of identifiable and acceptable tolerances. In engineering, these tolerances are sometimes infinitesimally small but nonetheless they are vitally important in making the difference between a triumph and a disaster.

You might like to ask yourself how you have reacted to things that almost went horribly wrong; to the near misses and close calls that all of us experience now and then. Are you confident that you know what you would have done in the event that the outcome had not been successful? Would you have had a plan B, an action plan and the resources to deal with a different outcome, or were you so confident that you assumed that it was bound to have been successful? Calculated risks need to be backed up by well-prepared alternative plans and routines. But would your plan B or contingency plan be prescriptive or would it encourage initiative, experimentation and risk taking by those closest to the seat of the problem when it arose?

What have you learned from such experiences?

If you were ever to experience something like such an event again, what might you do differently?

Summing up the points made so far in this chapter, we are suggesting that, as a leader, you will set the tone for your organization but that you carry the obligation to ensure that this tone is positive. You can only do this if you are mindful of the underlying attitudes, values and beliefs that shape your behavior and which in turn will come to shape values and beliefs that are held by others in your organization.

Recent developments in cognitive psychology suggest that, no matter what we may believe about our objectivity and our personal autonomy, many of our responses to events are largely a matter of the habitual ways of thinking and behaving that we have developed over the course of our lifetimes. We tend to see the world as we expect to see it rather than as it really is.

3.6   Check your assumptions

"Look busy! The boss is coming," is a comment that might well be overheard from among the members of a group of bored and under-utilized employees. The boss, seeing them working away busily , might be fooled into assuming that all is well, thus ensuring that their boring, unproductive jobs are maintained for a little longer. Alternatively, she may recognize the "game" that is being played here and ignore it as a fact of organizational life, thereby colluding in maintaining the mutual disrespect that exists between her and the group. The members of the group may assume that the boss is easily fooled, doesn't care or believes that it is inevitable that their work should be boring and that this is just the way things are. An overdependence on such long held expectations may cause both the manager and the group members to fail to notice the symptoms or to take the trouble to gather the evidence of something being wrong.

Just possibly, she might confront the group (without aggression) asking its members questions about what it is that they are doing, seeking evidence of their output and coming to acknowledge the shared waste of time, effort and self-esteem that their experience represents. She might engage the group in a discussion of how things could be improved. She might even confront the possibility that the group is over-resourced and that a change involving some difficult negotiations may prove to be necessary.

Whatever reaction she displays will be noted. Stories will be told about it, be modified, changed and enriched until they are incorporated into the organization's mythology. There, they will help determine the way in which the members of the organization perceive themselves and their leaders and eventually will become incorporated into the corporate culture.

John asserts that his engineering background and experience has caused him to develop his deeply held belief that business decisions need to be grounded on a foundation of rigorous analysis. "It's a matter of self discipline", he says, "Of course you can always overdo it. We have all met people who suffer from analysis paralysis and never seem to get to the point of making any decisions at all. But such paralysis probably only arises when just about everything is already out of kilter. It is as likely to have as much to do with a distaste for risk-taking as it has to do with a passion for analysis. What I am talking about is a willingness on the part of top managers to demand evidence and to be ready to challenge bullshit."

Unfortunately the higher reaches of a great many organizations appear to be immersed in a good deal of bullshit of their own creation. Beneath its weight, business leaders are invited to make decisions and initiate action. Such decisions may end up being based on information that is beautifully presented but inadequately tested; resting more upon opinion than upon fact and where the language employed obscures the inadequacy of the content. When things are going well and you and your colleagues are surfing the wave of euphoria that has been generated by your success is when you are likely to be most vulnerable.

The sycophantic courtier has been a significant character in the literature of tragedy, from the time of the ancient Greeks, through Shakespeare to the more recent plays of the late Harold Pinter, Tom Stoppard and David Hare. The character remains alive, well and active among senior managers and in today's boardrooms. Information is still all too often elegantly presented in terms that the presenter hopes will please the organization's leadership, emphasizing that which it is felt the leaders would like to be true and sweetening and mollifying that which is likely to be less pleasing to their ears.

John again:

> I accept that when you are dealing with marketing, customer relations and with potential sales commitments, you are dealing with much softer data than I was used to handling as an engineer. I also accept, of course, that the margins for error must necessarily be broader. You will often find yourself dealing with fine judgments, attitudes and opinions. But this doesn't mean that you should be any less rigorous in the ways in which you interpret such data. I would argue that, when you are in the role of a business or organizational leader you must, if anything, be even more rigorous in the way that you deal with soft data – precisely because it is so much more sensitive to interpretation.

We have noted earlier that dependence on the objectively quantifiable and measurable can be taken too far. Recent reliance on the achievement of numerical or quantifiable targets in matters of public education and health in the UK public sector appears to have been increasingly at the cost of losing touch with the original purposes that schools and hospitals were meant to serve. Often they appear to focus almost exclusively on that which is quantifiable rather than on that which is valuable.

Perhaps this is simply because the first is measurable while the second is always open to question and debate. But qualitative goals can be just as important as quantitative targets. They should not be neglected simply because they are more difficult to assess. It is simply a matter of acknowledging that their rigorous evaluation is going to be much more of a challenge – but that it is still just as necessary as the achievement of a numerical target and possibly more so.

3.7 The role of myths and stories

In marketing, brand building, customer relations or sales, you are dealing with attitudes, opinions and emotions on a grand scale. Part of the appeal of working in these areas is that they represent a world that is as full of stories, myths and legends as are the tales of King Arthur, Harry Potter and the Lord of the Rings. Please don't misunderstand us. We are not saying that this is a bad thing. Organizations thrive on their myths and stories, but they may also be dragged down by them.

We want to emphasize that it is an important part of your role as your organization's leader to be aware of its myths and stories and to ensure that those that are associated with you and with the actions that you take are to the organization's benefit. You also need to develop your understanding of those that are positive, understand why and modify your behavior appropriately, so that you can build upon them. You can only accomplish this if your leadership behavior provides the material upon which more positive stories and myths can develop and build.

Campaigns can be based on the story of a delighted customer telephoning her praises to the managing director, or on another tale concerning a competitor's blunder that has opened up a rich seam of opportunity to be mined by your own company. Such stories make a useful contribution to the development of a positive company tone and culture. But while it is true that mighty oaks originate from tiny acorns, it is equally true that the bindweed that ends up choking your favorite shrub to death springs from an insignificant little root. Myths and stories can be a powerful force for organizational cohesion and strength. They can also set in concrete an unjustified, hubristic self-belief that can be the cause of your organization's downfall – and of your own – unless you recognize and deal with them appropriately.

Stories and myths can be the starting point for what may turn out to be disasters or they may go on to lead you to unimagined success. But, either way, the hypotheses and assumptions that they encourage need to be brought out into the open, tested and subjected to objective criticism and evaluation.

For example, we have both experienced companies in which the contributions of their sales and marketing teams to corporate hospitality and entertainment have become legendary. Customers certainly loved these events but we have found it virtually impossible to determine just what it was that they contributed toward their companies' revenue and profit levels. They certainly provided a warm and pleasant atmosphere in which it became easy to do deals. But they also appear to have developed a tendency to become millstones around the necks of their CEOs. To have reduced them in scale or to have got rid of them altogether was seen by their top managers as being likely to suggest to their regular attendees that the company was in trouble, thus triggering yet another, less positive, myth or story about it.

Nevertheless, it has been difficult to for us to convince ourselves beyond any doubt that such events have really represented value for money as far as the host companies were concerned, rather than simply maintaining pleasant but unrealistic expectations on the part of both the companies and their customers. Either way, they make a contribution to the tone of the organization.

3.4 Consistent messages?

Message 1: At a company's recent sales conference, the managing director addressed the assembled sales force with an earnest tale of the difficult times lying ahead, of shrinking markets, tougher targets and the need for everyone to "tighten their belts." At the same time, he roused their enthusiasm with a quietly stated expression of his humility in the face of the wonderful commitment and loyalty that the sales force was continuing to display "both to me and to the company that we all serve." He trusted them, he said, to pull out all the stops and was fully confident that his team of champions would emerge as winners when the difficult period was over.

He went on to say that he also knew that they would all understand that the sumptuous dinner that he usually offered them at such conferences would be inappropriate in the present circumstances. He hoped, however, that they would enjoy the barbecue that he had arranged for them on the lawns of the conference center. In the spirit of his message he knew too that they would appreciate his being unable to join them as he needed to attend a vital meeting between the company's finance and marketing directors and the company's bankers.

He received a positive if somewhat less than rapturous response from his audience.

Unfortunately for the credibility of his message, the magnificent private dining room provided for him and his guests by the conference hotel happened to be in full view of those enjoying the barbecue. So they witnessed the liberal amounts of champagne, the fine wines, the lobster and other gastronomic delights that were being served to the managing director and his guests, while they tucked into their chicken wings, burgers and sausages.

Message 2: In the autumn of 2008, it was reported in the world's media that the heads of the US's three largest auto manufacturers – GM, Ford and Chrysler – had flown to Washington to appear before Congress in order to appeal for the funds they claimed were necessary to enable them to survive the twin storms of the "Credit Crunch" and impending global recession. They flew from Detroit to the Capital in corporate jets and were collected at the airport to be driven to Capitol Hill in company limousines.

> After they had made their pitch, citing the thousands of jobs that were likely to be lost if any of their companies should be allowed to fail, a congressman asked them to raise their hands if, in return for being bailed out by the American taxpayer, they would be willing to give up their company jet.
>
> No hands were raised.

In this way are new myths born. We wonder whether the credibility of the managing director and the American automobile chiefs will bounce back from the impact that their messages provided. The fact that it was announced some days after the congressional hearings that one of the auto chiefs was giving up his jet, had much less impact than did the news of his flight to Washington. It is that flight that will go down in history.

Sometimes, it seems that the power of the tale or myth is stronger than the company leader's grip upon the facts. The wish that the myth be true can overwhelm both judgment and perceptions of reality.

A Japanese industrialist once suggested to us that the tendency to represent the world as they would like it to be, rather than as it is, is a deeply ingrained characteristic of Western business leaders. They look out, he said, for signs that suggest to them and to others that their vision is true, while giving much less attention to those signs that might threaten to deny such a belief. In contrast, their Japanese counterparts, said the industrialist, are much more comfortable with representing the world as it really is and then diligently seeking ways in which to transform it into something that they would like it to be.

In consequence, he argued, Japanese companies take a long time to come up with their initial plans for the introduction of a radically innovative product. But once the necessary planning has been completed (planning that is based upon rigorously gathered and thoroughly analysed data in which everybody believes), then the company will move like greased lightning from plan, through product development and to production.

In contrast, he suggested, their Western competitors have often been first to market with brilliant new products but have tended to lose momentum as they correct errors, and take longer to find the most appropriate market niche, so that the product ends up costing them a great deal more than originally expected and the reputation of its developers is damaged as a result.

Such generalizations are, of course, themselves based on myths and stories. But they do illustrate an important lesson: the corporate leader needs to be convinced that the world that is being presented to him is grounded in reality rather than in the wishful thinking of the marketing, brand builder, public relations, product development or other enthusiasts.

This isn't always easy. John points out that,

When I was a newly appointed managing director, I took the decision to slash our marketing budget by 50 percent because the marketing team was unable to demonstrate what return the company would be getting for its investment in it. This went very much against the grain of past practice. It didn't help that I also added that any expenditure of the revised budget would need to be supported by a sound business case that offered measures of the beneficial effects that such expenditure would have. That certainly made the members of the marketing team think, as well as curse me. But eventually it brought to the fore a different kind of marketing person. Instead of someone who based their working life around the planning and running of social events, dealer conferences and lavish entertainments, the requirement to identify specific and measurable outcomes brought forth marketers who were interested in collecting and interpreting data, in sorting out what was really going on and in calculating probabilities and risks before committing themselves to a particular program. Having done this and having convinced both themselves and me as their MD of the robustness of their case, they were able to drive ahead with a much greater sense of focus and confidence because they were working from a basis of evidence rather than from one of bluster and mutual admiration.

3.8   Honor the experts – wherever you find them

The complex and uncertain world of corporate leadership is increasingly dependent on access to all kinds of expertise that leaders could not possibly possess themselves. But it is important not to confuse such expertise with a broad intelligence. Expertise involves having the knowledge necessary to be able to determine what to do in a given set of circumstances. But it doesn't necessarily involve the ability to know how the expert knows what she knows nor that of being able to explain what she knows to somebody else who does not share her expertise.

Intelligence, on the other hand, as Jean Piaget suggests, involves, "knowing what to do when you don't know what to do."[6]

It seems to us that the recent mushrooming of the consultancy industry owes a great deal to a failure on the part of leadership and senior management. They have failed to take seriously their responsibility for ensuring that the decisions that they take are based on a rigorous analyses of which they themselves have a thorough understanding. We are not especially critical of management consultants, having both enjoyed and benefited from playing such roles over many years. But you can have too much of a good thing. The commissioning of a consultant often seems to us to have been an act of laziness, substituting a consultancy contract for the thinking that you should be doing for yourself and for knowledge and expertise that already resides untapped within your organization. Moreover, not all management consultants are good.

We certainly don't mean to imply that top management should make the time and have the expertise to undertake all the specialized or technical analyses that may be necessary to making decisions about the organization's future. Such analyses are the proper role and contribution of the expert, who may in turn need to be a consultant. But your responsibility as organizational leader is to ensure that such analyses are undertaken objectively and competently by external resources, only when you are genuinely convinced that you do not have access to such knowledge and expertise within your organization. You must also ensure that the analyses and proposals are communicated to you in a form that you can fully comprehend and that they are open to rigorous challenge and debate if you wish them to be taken seriously. Far too often, it seems to us, company boards and government ministers have been so seduced by the power of the consultants' brand image that they have failed to challenge or, in some cases, even to fully understand the consultants' recommendations and possible consequences.

If you are to deal successfully with the impact of unexpected events, a test of your leadership capability will be your willingness to defer to the expertise of others, wherever it may be located, while not compromising your leadership authority and accountability.

Similarly, it may help raise the morale of your staff for you to be present at the scene of a crisis and it may be necessary for the company's public relations. But make sure that your presence is appropriate. Empower the experts on the scene, give them your support but don't get in their way and don't make statements that may turn a crisis into a disaster.

By all means use consultants but insist that they fully justify and explain their recommended solutions to your problems or proposals in your terms rather than their own. After all it is you who will be picking up the bill – in every sense.

Companies need the inputs of specialist expertise, but it is their leaders' responsibility to take the final decisions – to have the intelligence to know what to do when they don't know what to do. They also require the intelligence and self-confidence to know when they need to ask for expert help and to recognize that such help may already lie within the organization, lower down the pyramid and close to where the unexpected occurrence may have had its earliest impact. The challenge is to have set a tone within the organization that enables this resource to have the confidence and courage to spring into action when required, rather than to wait for your direction or for the hiring of external consultants whose need to undertake their analyses postpones the requirement to make a decision that rests with you.

Remember, while you may have delegated your authority, you remain accountable. If the analyses upon which you base your decisions have also been assigned to consultants, then you run the risk of having abrogated your responsibility. Just because the consultant's brand is counted as world-class and their services are costing your business a king's ransom doesn't change the location of accountability one jot – it remains with you.

3.9 Leaders need to focus on solutions rather than on problems

Paul Jackson and Mark McKergow bring an unusual mix of experience to the matter of solving problems in business. Paul is a one-time journalist, university lecturer, trainer and comedy producer for BBC radio with an interest in family therapy. Mark has applied his Ph.D. in physics to working as a nuclear physicist in the electronics industry, while playing jazz saxophone and collecting an MBA along the way.

Perhaps it was the diversity of their knowledge and experience that enabled them to come up with the simple proposition that it is better to focus on solutions than on problems. From this proposition they have gone on to develop a practical method for putting this approach into practice.[7]

They argue that when you are dealing with complex problems it is likely that the solutions too will be complex. Therefore, you should direct your attention toward seeking the solution rather than adding to the complexity of the situation by focusing primarily on the problem. Focusing on the solution rather than the problem is totally relevant to the matter of managing the unexpected. Jackson and McKergow start by suggesting that you should find out what is working well and do more of it and that you should stop doing what doesn't work and do something else. This sounds simple because it is. It is the fact that these principles need to be applied in situations that are complex, dynamic and subject to multiple and subtle sources of change that provides the challenge in their approach.

They suggest that you should focus on:

- The future — not on the past
- What's working — not on what's not working
- On making progress — not on assigning blame
- On influencing action — not on controlling action
- On collaborating with experts — not on depending on them
- On resources — not on deficiencies
- On areas of simplicity — not on those of complexity
- On actions — not on definitions

In general terms, these little homilies are helpful, but we feel that we need to add some words of caution here. Concentrating on areas of simplicity makes sense at the site of the problem, where it may be necessary in order to simplify things so that those tasked with coming up with a solution may remain focused on a limited number of critical issues. You are responsible for enabling them to have the space do this. But as a leader of the organization your role is somewhat different from theirs. You need to simplify less in order to be able to see more. At the top of the organization, Karl Weick and Kathleen Sutcliffe point out, you role is to "integrate a myriad simplified tasks", and by reviewing them in their wider context, to remain in touch with their complexity.[8] Simplify at the point of the problem but be sure that you do not simplify so much that you lose touch with its wider context.

If, as a leader, you oversimplify things, you run the risk of reducing the number of things that you notice.

3.10 Surfacing your attitudes – some key questions

Setting the tone for an organization requires you to assert yourself in the leadership role and demands that you are ready and willing to make uncomfortable choices that are bolstered by the self-knowledge and self-awareness that you have ensured that you possess. This requires that you understand your own role in generating the stories and myths on which your organization will either thrive or flounder. People become as good or as bad as you tell them and as they think they are.

You need to look beyond your pet projects and beyond the boundaries of your organization in order to be sensitive to the trends and disturbances that are going on out there and which may come to be the cause of unexpected events that may knock your cherished projects off track. When such events do occur, be prepared to seek out the help of expertise that is relevant to the area in which the event and its associated problems have arisen. Seek help but never ever forget that it is you who is accountable. Encourage your experts to focus on solutions and to keep things simple rather than on explaining problems. At the same time, ensure you remain in touch with the bigger picture, keep in touch with the environment's complexity and that you do not allow simplification to become simplistic.

So, here are some more questions:

- How confident are you in the quality of the information that is provided to you when things are going wrong?
- How do you deal with errors or mistakes?
  (a) Your own?
  (b) Those made by other people?
- What is your characteristic response to a challenge – are you more likely to see it as a threat or as an opportunity?
- How would you react if a junior colleague were to question or challenge one of your ideas or plans?
  (a) In private?
  (b) In public?
- How do you respond to new ideas from people lower down the organization?
  Are you inclined to respond, "Yes, but ..."
  or, "Yes, and ..."
- How easy do you find it to ask for help?
- How do you manage your poor performers?
- When you take a calculated risk and it comes off, are you more likely to feel that you have chalked up another personal success or that you have "got away with it"? Do you review what really

happened in order to learn for next time? Do you thank your lucky stars and move on?

- Do you tend to look for culprits, search for solutions, or both?
- How widely would you share the information that something unexpected has happened?
  Would you:
  (a) Limit it to those who need to know so that everyone else can carry on as usual and not worry about it?
  (b) Inform as many as people as possible in the hope that they will be alerted to the possibility of similar events occurring in the future?
- How often do you engage consultants?
- For what purposes?
- Do you know whether or not your organization already possesses the knowledge and skills offered to you by external experts?
- What is it that you are buying from consultants?
- To what extent do you focus on problems rather than on their solutions?

CHAPTER 4

No surprises! – anticipating and preparing for the unexpected

Feelings of surprise are diagnostic because they are a solid cue that one's model of the world is flawed
Karl Weick and Kathleen Sutcliffe[1]

4.1 Any bus can take you there

As an organizational leader you are operating at the interface between the past, the present and the future. If you are to manage this interface effectively, you are going to need the ability to appreciate the past, to understand the present and to anticipate, plan for and shape the future. A core message of this book is that the plans that you make for that future will be constantly and increasingly buffeted by unexpected events with the potential to knock such plans for six.

By definition, the nature, location and the timing of these events are unknown. But simply because specific unexpected events cannot be precisely forecast does not mean that the probability of such events occurring cannot be anticipated and prepared for.

The first step in such preparation is a highly personal one. As we first suggested in Chapter 3, it involves you as a leader in being very clear about who you are, what you stand for, what you believe in and precisely what it is that you wish to make happen. If you are unclear about these things and where you wish to be, you are likely to find yourself taken somewhere else by the first bus that happens to come along. You are also likely to find that more and more of your time and that of others in your organization will need to be spent, as was noted by the British prime minister, Harold Macmillan in the early 1960s, dealing with, "events, dear boy, events."

In this chapter, we consider some of the basic elements that need to be involved in helping you to prepare for the unexpected and the groundwork that you will need to do, both personally and with the support of organizational colleagues at many different levels. We suggest ways in which you can help yourself to identify touchstones, the fixed points that are of fundamental importance to you when dealing with the unfamiliar and the unexpected – fixed points that must remain in place if you are not to be knocked off-track and prevented from seizing unexpected opportunities or dealing appropriately with an unexpected crisis.

We go on to consider ways in which the weak signals that may presage unexpected events and which can so easily be overlooked, might be amplified or made more visible through the generation of "memories of the future." We take a preliminary look at various ways of responding to unexpected events that will help you towards continuously improving your capacity to anticipate such events in the future. Finally, we raise some more questions, which we suggest you should be asking yourself as part of your own preparation for encounters with the unexpected.

4.2   Doing the groundwork: personal integrity

4.1   Remember who you are!

A story is told concerning the late satirist and comedian, Peter Cook. Early in his career he was one of the owners and a star performer at the 'The Establishment' nightclub. The story goes that one night, when Cook was in the middle of performing to a packed house, a minor American celebrity arrived at the entrance and demanded to be admitted, notwithstanding the "House Full" signs. When the hapless person on the door refused to let him in, the visitor became very angry shouting, "Do you know who I am?" Cook heard the shouts and stopped in the middle of his act saying, "I wonder if there is anyone in the audience who can help. There is a gentleman at the door who appears not to know who he is." The audience howled with mirth and the luckless gentleman departed from the scene somewhat sheepishly.

There is a serious point to be made here.

We all reflect the personal history and experiences that have gone to shape our values, our attitudes and our beliefs. As we noted in Chapter 3, this process has been going on since the day we were born. We pick them up from our families, from our communities, from our education and from our personal experiences and those that we have shared with others. We also develop them from the roles that we are called upon to play.

But because this is a constant and ongoing process, we can easily lose sight of how we come to hold the particular values, attitudes and beliefs that we do and of the fact that some of them are likely to be inconsistent with one another. We manage such inconsistencies by compartmentalizing the roles that we play. For example, by behaving quite differently as a partner and parent from the ways that we behave as a director or a chief executive or on a "night out with the boys/girls."

The former chief executive of Scandinavian Airlines, SAS, Jan Carlzon[2] tells that when he was first appointed to the position of president of one of the airline's subsidiaries, he exhausted himself by trying to be what he thought the role demanded, attempting to appear highly dynamic, trying to control everything around him, barking instructions because, he said, he thought that this was what a chief executive was "supposed to do." Fortunately for him, a junior manager in the organization, but one who seems to have acted as a mentor to him on his way up the career ladder, came to see him and told him that he was behaving like an idiot. He had been appointed because of who and what he already was not because of some impression that he held of what a chief executive ought to be. "Remember who you are," was the manager's sound advice for which Carlzon was extremely grateful. He calmed down, relaxed into the role and went on to be instrumental in transforming the airline from a loss-maker to one that, under his leadership, became highly profitable.

Carlzon comments :

> The company was not asking me to make all the decisions on my own, only to create the right atmosphere, the right conditions for others to do their jobs better.

He goes on to describe the role of the corporate leader as being that of someone who must, "set the tone and keep the big picture in mind." Precisely our point.

In the excitement and, perhaps, the euphoria of reaching the top of your particular career ladder, it is tempting to focus on the things that you are going to do now that you are there. Many years ago, management guru Tom Peters stated that successful companies demonstrate "a bias for action."[3] This may be the case for successful companies but does the same apply to successful leaders? As the managing director of an international software development company told us:

4.2   Dancing on hot coals

I had been frustrated in my previous role because I felt that I knew what needed to be done to get the business moving in the right direction but I didn't have the power or the authority to make it happen. When I came out of the chairman's office having been offered and accepted the role of MD, my first thought was; *"Now I'll make the buggers dance!"* But that feeling didn't last very long. I soon realized that I needed to think through what kind of managing director I needed to be if I wanted the vision that I had for the business become a reality. I was going to need a lot of

> help and the people whose help I needed would only do
> so if they wanted to help me, the person, not me, the MD.
> Making them dance on metaphorical hot coals wasn't going
> to achieve that.

You cannot depend on the arrival of someone who cares about
you sufficiently to hold up the mirror to you, as was the case
with Jan Carlzon, or on having the level of self-insight of the
managing director of the software company. When taking on
the role of leader, you will find yourself carrying not only your
own expectations but facing the many and varied expectations
of a host of other people as well. Many of these expectations are
likely to be quite unrealistic.

The initial focus of attention of the software company's MD was
on what she was going to do now that she was boss. But you need to
pay as much attention to what is going on around you right now as
you do to the strategies and plans that you may have for the future.
Those plans too need to be thought through and you also need to
ask yourself whether they are based on little more than extrapola-
tions of present conditions that may not apply in the future.

Asking yourself the following questions might prove to be
salutary:

- How well do I know what's going on?
- Do my managers and my advisors know what's going on?
- Do my expectations and my behaviors encourage them to tell
  me what's going on – even when they may suspect that I will
  not like what's going on?
- Do I actively encourage them to find out what's going on?
- How often do I ask them what's going on?

Then ask yourself:

- How will I know that my answers to such questions are
  accurate?
- How in touch am I with trends and events in the outside world
  that may have an impact on the plans that I am making?

4.3 Managing by exception or merely missing the signals?

Many of us, fearing that we might become guilty of micromanaging, have become accustomed to managing by exception – being confident that things are going well unless they are reported as otherwise. The night watchmen of old London are remembered for their regular hourly call, announcing, "Eleven O'clock and all's well!" This was very comforting to the city's citizens as they settled down for the night. But how well-informed were the watchmen? How well-informed could they be unless others were monitoring what was going on in the streets around them and regularly updating them?

Management by exception may be appropriate in highly stable situations that run along in line with your expectations. But unless you were alert to the fact that the night watchman hadn't cried out, "All's well!," you were unlikely to be prepared for the burglars who had mugged him and who were now breaking into your home. In other words, there are many circumstances in which management by exception can be misleading and when there are very good reasons for your not being told that things are not going to plan. For example, when you have forgotten to switch on your Blackberry or mobile phone; when your regular informant has gone sick or has been delayed; when you had told your personal assistant that you were not to be disturbed.

Keeping yourself fully apprised of what is going on in the organization is costly in terms of time, effort and of money. If you are fully confident that your business is one of those rare ones in which everything that happened yesterday is likely to happen today, and just as likely to be repeated tomorrow, and that if things were to turn out differently you would be quite happy, confident that there would be sufficient slack in the system to take care of the disturbance, then management by exception is for you! But if you are not in this unusually lucky situation, then you and your organizational colleagues need to have a pretty clear idea of the things that you simply cannot allow to go wrong and to know exactly what would need to be done if and when they do go wrong – as one day they will.

Management by exception is only partially helpful here. In an uncertain environment you need to enlarge the range of what people expect, what they are constantly looking out for and what they fear could happen.

4.4   Values, attitudes and beliefs

Here again your values, your attitudes and your beliefs provide the screen or filter through which you view the world. They shape your expectations and, as we considered in the previous chapter, they go a long way to determining the things that you will notice as you go through life, and those that are likely to pass you by. These things are those that tend to confirm your values, attitudes and beliefs.

If you wish to be prepared for the unexpected, it will be helpful to you to make sure that you are in touch with just what these values, attitudes and beliefs happen to be. Even though they have been built up over the course of a lifetime, they are not set in stone and may be modified, adjusted or updated if you so wish and if you are willing to take the time and trouble to understand them and what they may mean to the way that you fulfill your leadership role. If you are unable to take the time for yourself to enable you to examine and question them, you are likely to find yourself "explaining" the occurrence of an unexpected event in terms of your beliefs about what you wish were true about it rather than in terms of the facts of the situation. You are more likely to ask whose fault it was, to seek out whom to blame, rather than to learn from it and to discover how to avoid it happening again.

Such examination involves an act of what the management writer, Charles Handy, has called "proper selfishness." He describes how when he was a young man he always wanted to be something else – a great athlete, a businessman, the head of a major institution. In fact he went through life as most of us do, "happier going along with the conventions of the time, measuring success in terms of money and position, climbing ladders which others placed in my way, collecting things and contacts rather than giving expression to my own personality."[4]

In other words, writes Handy, he was not only concerned with turning himself into someone else but also with acquiring the "symbols and labels" that indicated that he really was such a person. Proper selfishness, argues Handy, involves you in becoming more fully aware of the person you already are and of the impact that the beliefs and the values that you hold have upon others. It is this that determines the ways in which they will relate and respond to you in the longer term. As a leader of an organization, unless you are sufficiently comfortable to allow your true self to be visible, you will only be playing a part and when you forget your lines, your credibility will fly out of the window.

It would be as well for you as a leader to remember this since you will only achieve your goals if others feel that they are worth pursuing and that you are someone for whom they have sufficient respect to enable them to identify both with you and with the goals that you are inviting them to share.

But, neither Handy nor the authors suggest that as a leader of your organization you should lock yourself away in order to submit yourself to prolonged periods of introspection and navel gazing. You are much more likely to gain an insight into who you really are from reflecting on the ways in which you have responded to unexpected events or crises in the past – events such as not being appointed to a job on which you had set your heart, having an accident, an experience of redundancy or near-death, of being badly let down, or of grabbing an opportunity and making a success of it.

4.3 Do you need a crisis?

Graham asked the vice president of the European region of a major multinational company whether the time he had spent reflecting on a recent financial crisis had changed the way in which he carried out his role. He replied, *"Yes, I think so.*

> *I think there's got to be some crisis to make you stop and think. It doesn't have to be that – but there's got to be something that pulls you up. Otherwise you just carry on because you work on adrenaline and, in the end, that's all you know and that's all you do."*

The point is to consider the shock that such an event provides to your system and to consider what made you respond to it in the particular way that you did. What beliefs were involved? What values were threatened or confirmed? How did your sense of personal integrity emerge from the experience? How did you feel? What might you have done differently? How did others regard your response? How did it affect their responses to you? Above all – What did you learn?

In this way, you will find that you begin to develop a clearer sense of those beliefs that you hold that are fundamental to the real you rather than the beliefs that you might expect someone in your role to hold, or that you feel that such a person ought to hold. You may also identify those beliefs and values that have outlived their usefulness but which leap to the surface when you are struck by something unexpected. In so doing, you begin to highlight the fixed points that are critical to you, looking beyond the role of leader that you happen to be occupying at the moment, to the person, the human being that you are and as you are seen to be by others.

4.5   Doing the groundwork: organizational integrity

4.5.1   The role of policy and procedure

Policies and procedures provide essential frameworks for determining how things should be done, both when things are running smoothly and when the circumstances are exceptional. But you should always remember that they can never anticipate the specific details of a particular unexpected event. They may tell you to ensure that all ladders are secured and what to do when one or two are found to have been left insecure. But they cannot tell you precisely which one you should deal with first or how to handle the contingent problems and other eventualities that may arise as a result of one's having been left unsecured.

4.4 Mistakes are made by people – not by procedures

In the autumn of 2008 the tragic case came to light and into the media headlines of a London toddler who had been abused over many months by his mother, stepfather and their lodger. Eventually the child died of his multiple injuries. It emerged that the childcare authorities had long been aware that the child was at serious risk of the abuse that eventually killed him. Its staff had visited him and the family on numerous occasions but had for a variety of reasons not intervened to save his life.

Responding to the public and media's sense of horror and outrage, the head of Children's Services who was responsible for the provision of the support that might have saved the child's life appeared on television. She gave a thoroughly professional presentation of the investigations that were currently underway to determine whether or not the appropriate procedures had been properly followed.

The presentation was a public relations disaster. People wanted to see a human being showing that she felt, or at least empathized, with the emotions that they were experiencing; someone who was as sorry, upset and as distressed as they were. Instead they saw the role rather than the person – a professional, cold and aloof – and this made them even angrier than they already were.

Later it became apparent that the concern with following the correct procedures and processes appeared to have been linked to a matching concern with meeting government targets and with filing reports. Somewhere along the line it seemed that the protection of a vulnerable child had gone missing.

Had the media misrepresented the head of Children's Services by editing out her apology as was later alleged?

We do not know the answer. Whatever the truth may be, the case offers a stark warning. Do not enter the lion's den without adequate preparation and protection. Lions play by their own rules.

In preparing to meet the unexpected, leaders of organizations need to take a long hard look at their policies and procedures and ask themselves some searching questions about them, but they must never forget that beyond the policies, the processes and the procedures, they remain a human being in relationships with other human beings who include the media and members of the public.

Policies and procedures become dangerous when they are seen as prescriptions rather than as providing guidance towards appropriate action. The example given above of serious failings in the field of a social services organization showed that the head of Children's Services had missed the point when she stated that she was investigating to ensure that the appropriate procedures had been followed. That, surely, was secondary to the fact that there had been a tragic failure for which she as the senior person involved was accountable, since it had occurred "on her watch." Investigation of the level of adherence to policies and procedures, while clearly necessary, should not detract from acceptance of that accountability. This was something that she appeared to have overlooked when making her televised statement.

Policies, procedures and targets can lead you to focus on levels of success that are to be determined by the extent to which the organization adheres to such frameworks. When these frameworks become highly complex and routinized, such conformance risks becoming an end in itself:

> The operation was a complete success. Unfortunately, however, the patient died.

In the case described above, a subsequent investigation revealed that the authority had been highly rated in the quality of its child protection services by an earlier, independent review. But that review had been based to a great extent on the evidence of statistical returns and on the analysis of performance against quantifiable targets. There had been little or no examination or spot checks of what was actually happening to vulnerable children in the community.

Procedures and targets may cause people to focus exclusively on levels of success rather than to concern themselves with the possibility of failure. In isolation, investigation of whether or not procedures have been followed may smack of seeking where the blame might lie rather than accepting responsibility for the occurrence of a tragic event.

As the leader of your organization you will fully appreciate that goals and targets are vital. But you should try to encourage a mindset where people look beyond the rules and procedures and develop a concern for what it might mean when they are broken or when something happens that causes them to be missed or ignored. Try to avoid (and challenge when you find that it already exists) the mindset within which people prefer to follow rules and procedures blindly, without question and without attention to the human context within which they are operating.

Such a mindset may lead them to shoehorn the implications of experiences that do not readily fit their expectations into the framework that the rules provide. This can provide an excuse to stay within their comfort zone rather than acting appropriately to the demands of an unexpected situation. This is equivalent to continuing to run on cruise control when a hazard appears on the horizon. Such a mindset works to conceal error and thus to build up problems for the future.

Errors and unexpected events will occur. It is the role of the leader to take responsibility for their consequences and to ensure that the organization is not disabled by them. If it is, then the leader must carry the consequences. So, while we recognize that providing effective leadership may involve you in temporarily handing over the reins of leadership to those with greater relevant expertise, regardless of their status and seniority, it also requires you to recognize and to be comfortable with the fact that the buck still remains firmly with you.

You must ensure that you are constantly alert for the possibility of failure anywhere in the organization and encourage this as a concern that is shared by everyone else in the organization. Don't misunderstand us. We are not suggesting for a moment that you should become an organizational Cassandra, preaching doom, gloom and impending disaster. But that, just as you should be properly selfish, you should expect that that which can go wrong is likely to go wrong – unless you are constantly on the lookout for the possibility of its going wrong. Sensitize yourself to the signals of error and failure rather than simply focusing on the achievement of targets and other measures of success.

Just as there is a risk that the organization that punishes mistakes causes them to be hidden rather than acknowledged, so the organization that focuses on quantifiable measures of success encourages the "enrichment" of data from which such measures of success are derived. You tend to find what you wish to find.

The policies and procedures of many organizations serve as monuments to the past rather than as performance tools that people are accustomed to using every day. Policies need to be living, evolving things that serve as guidance for action rather than as barriers to initiative and creativity. As such they need to be subjected to constant review and to be adapted and developed in the light of changing circumstances so that they can prepare the organization and its members for those exceptional situations that require a considered response. But they can never offer a total solution.

A company's policy structure determines what it means to be "playing at home." When you are telephoned by a tabloid journalist with the request that you comment on the developing story that one of your colleagues has been accused of insider trading, what will you do? After all, the colleague may be a close friend on whom you have depended for many years and who has shared with you the good and the bad times. You are bumping up against potentially conflicting values and beliefs.

Your response should be guided by well thought out policies (on yours and the company standards on the one hand and on dealing with the press on the other). If you fail to do this, worse still if you have no prepared policy to guide you, it is likely that you will find yourself "playing away from home,"' that is, reacting emotionally from your heart and playing by the journalist's rules rather than by those that are guided by your head, by policy and by the interests of your business. All too often directors and managers fall victim to this trap in the heat of the moment. They flail around in unfamiliar territory and lose control of the situation. Journalists recognize this possibility all too well and will, therefore, address your ego rather than risk finding that they are blocked by your company's policies. They know that they are much more likely to get a good story that way, so:

Be human but play by the rules – play by the rules but stay human.

Newly appointed organizational leaders would do well to immerse themselves very early on in their organization's policies, identifying those areas that are at odds with their personal attitudes, values and aspirations for their organization. Where such disconnections are shown to exist, something will have to change if the leader, the organization or both are not to be put at risk when the unexpected happens as, inevitably, it will. As a leader you need to ensure that such change is well planned and well managed. It must not be allowed to come about by default.

Policies become bureaucratic and irrelevant when they simply reflect the past rather than providing ground rules for the present and guidelines for future action in a wide variety of situations and circumstances that may be unpredictable. They should focus on principles, offering clear guidance rather than prescriptions, and provide a framework within which managers can find a route through the apparently random and chaotic territory that is occupied by modern organizations. Procedures can afford to be more prescriptive (because their application is likely to be more limited) stating the behaviors that are required in specific and strictly defined circumstances – such as when the fire alarm sounds.

4.6   Doing the groundwork: aligning resources

The most relevant expertise upon which you are going to depend is likely to be located close to the seat of operational knowledge and experience. Therefore, the development of policies and procedures also needs to take place as close to their area of application as possible, if their relevance to practice is to be ensured. This needs to be reflected in those policies and procedures developed to provide guidance for action in the wake of an unexpected event in areas as diverse as:

- People
- Operations
- Maintenance
- Finance
- Communication
- Innovation
- Risk
- Recovery etc.

Karl Weick and Kathleen Sutcliffe[5] point out that those who are routinely engaged in maintenance work tend to occupy relatively low positions on the organizational pyramid but, because they are regularly dealing with the consequences of failures, errors and the unexpected, they have a good sense for picking up the weak signals that can indicate that such an event is about to happen. However, these people may not speak up about what they have seen and heard because they are of the view that it is not their place or their responsibility or, worse still, that no one will listen to them so that there is no point. You need to be sure that the organization and managerial culture doesn't support them in this view by suggesting to them that it is correct.

Everyone in the organization needs to feel responsible for listening, noticing and seeking out signs of failure so that they can "secure the unsecured ladder."

It is down to organizational leaders to ensure that they make available sufficient time and space to enable this to happen – time both for themselves and for others who may well have expectations that are quite different from their own.

Weick and Sutcliffe note that a great many organizations demonstrate a tendency towards mindlessness that is characterized "by a style of mental functioning in which people follow recipes, impose old categories to classify what they see, act with some rigidity, operate on automatic pilot, and mislabel unfamiliar new contexts as familiar old ones. A mindless mental state works to conceal problems that are worsening."[6]

This comes down to being a failure of leadership.

Preparing for the unexpected is a very good reason for conducting a post mortem when an error or unexpected event has occurred. This cannot be limited to discovering whether or not the proper procedures have been followed. Such a course of action suggests a bias towards prejudging that failure to follow procedures has been the most likely cause of the problem and reduces the attention that is given to other possibilities. It also implies an approach that is primarily concerned with identifying "the guilty."

As we have already noted a climate within which people expect to be punished for their mistakes is hardly likely to be one where they will readily admit to them. Their energies are more likely to be diverted into concealing them than to acknowledging them openly and contributing enthusiastically to seeking ways to rectify the error.

Jim Collins puts it well:

> When you conduct autopsies without blame, you go a long way to creating a climate where the truth is heard. If you have the right people on the bus, you should almost never need to assign blame, but need only to search for understanding and learning.[7]

In a nutshell, policies and procedures need to facilitate action that is appropriate in unfamiliar situations rather than to constrain it within the boundaries of the familiar. After all, rules are general while every situation is unique, even though it may very well possess some familiar characteristics. It is a case of finding the right balance between sufficient prescription to provide a clear framework for action and providing adequate local discretion to ensure that the action that is taken is appropriate to the particular circumstances.

The first stages of the groundwork involved in anticipating the unexpected are complete when you as the leader of the organization have sufficient knowledge, awareness and insight to give you confidence that you and your organization's goals, values, plans, policies, programs and projects are well aligned, that they are coherent and that they make sense in the particular context within which you are operating. But this is only the first step on the road. You need to be constantly monitoring, listening and heeding the signals that indicate that change is on the way. Then you need to ensure that such change takes place appropriately. This requires you to be sensitive to the future.

4.7   Seeking signals, telling stories

Numerous tools are available to organizational leaders to assist them to anticipate the unexpected. These may be relatively informal and individual, or formal, sophisticated, complex and which require the involvement of many people. But each needs time, space and a degree of tranquility to enable you to seek out the clues to the unexpected that they may reveal. This is at odds with the frenetic pace of modern business and represents yet another challenge to organizational leaders. They are expected to demonstrate a bias for action, for making things happen and for getting things done. But action is useless unless it is effective. Only too often, ill thought out actions are proven to be merely a reflection of a "'ready, fire, aim" approach to leading.

If leaders are to make sense of the unexpected they must keep in touch with the wider context within which their businesses operate. They must see to it that their thinking extends beyond the boundaries of their organization, its industry and market sector and out into its wider socio-economic, political, cultural and technological environment. It is out here that the sources of the

major unexpected events that challenge organizational performance often originate.

We are not suggesting that your strategic vision of the future
should be all encompassing. We are saying that you need to
ensure that you are tuned into what is going on in the world
around you right now and to be sensitive to the clues and messages that it offers you and your business about things that might
significantly affect it – either positively or negatively – but which
may not have been built into your strategies and plans.

Time for asking, "what if …?" is critical, but is often very difficult to find.

Quiet reflection is often regarded with suspicion as though
it were not quite proper; not "real" work. But it too is vitally
important.

4.5   Who was the doctor?

In the early 1960s, the heroic or notorious Dr Beeching
(depending on your perspective) was commissioned by the
government of the day to develop a plan for the future of Britain's railways. His notoriety stemmed for the fact that he was
willing to think the unthinkable in order to reduce dramatically
the number of routes and services offered by the railways, far
beyond both the dreams of his sponsors and the worst expectations of his strongest critics. His plan reflected his consideration of social and economic trends, extrapolated into a distant
future in which he anticipated increasing affluence, a dramatic
growth in commercial road traffic and private motoring and
a vision of a significant shift in the needs and expectations of
the railways that very few others at that time shared.

What particularly interests us about Dr Beeching is the
manner in which he worked for much of the time. It is said
that he would enter his office, remove his shoes, sit behind
his enormous, empty desk and place his feet in its equally
empty bottom drawer. Once settled in this location, he would
seem to disappear into a trance like state for considerable

---

periods of time, during which he would visualize a range of "possible futures." He would then work his way back from these "futures" to the present day, examining as he went the implications for the railways of the day and the role they would play in the future that he envisioned. But others around him complained that he was being paid a fortune for sitting and daydreaming. They seriously questioned the sanity of his appointment.

This is, perhaps, an early example of a basic and somewhat idiosyncratic version of the tool of scenario planning which is now routinely employed by many organizations to help them in the development of their long-term strategies and plans.

Arie de Geus[8], who as head of group planning was responsible for introducing scenario planning to Shell International, describes it as a "technique well suited for building memories of the future." The "what if" question is writ large here because the process involves thinking about the unthinkable or, at least, the unlikely.

The phrase "memories of the future" is important because memories are stored and can be recalled and, in the case of scenario planning, they are widely shared. As we have noted, when confronted with the unexpected, the human brain searches for something like it that is stored in the memory, eradicating unlikely matches before they rise to consciousness. To have stored "memories" of the future in the context of which an unexpected event then occurs is likely to provide a powerful stimulus to recalling them when they are needed. The fact that such memories are shared only goes to strengthen this process.

Arie de Geus' use of the plural, "memories", here is extremely important. Scenarios are outline sketches of several different possible futures that offer alternatives to the commonsense or preferred views of the future that are set out in conventional plans and strategies. Such plans tend to start from where things are, panning out from there towards some desirable future state.

Scenario planning operates the other way around by stepping outside your business, looking into the future for significant trends and then looking back to the organization to see what the implications of such trends might be for the performance of its business. When practised well the approach involves widely diverse groups of people from within an organization in looking at the world in which the business is operating. The resulting scenarios need to be presented in a form that is sufficiently close to their own experience and to reflect a world that they recognize, or they will be seen as academic and irrelevant (and relevance is critical).

Moreover scenarios do not start from the perspective of what you might want the organization to be doing. This would be too limiting. No, scenario planners need to go out into the world beyond the confines of their organization and seek to identify the "driving forces" that are at work out there. Only then should they look back at their business and ask themselves what relevance such forces might possibly have for their business' future. The impact of such forces is likely to have a considerable range of possible and different consequences.

Scenarios are presented in the form of "stories" that describe these consequences in simple and straightforward terms and are presented in terms that are meaningful to other people in the company, capturing their imaginations and forming the basis for a series of wide ranging discussions that involve an equally wide range of people. They do not try to cover all or even most of the eventualities that might arise from the large number of "driving forces" that are constantly reshaping the context within which the business operates. To attempt to do so would be impossible. Instead they endeavor to convey a basic story of the implications that a few disparate but quite possible situations might have.

The stories that are told within organizations are a very important aspect of its tone and culture. This is why in the previous chapter we emphasized how important it is for leaders to recognize their personal obligation for setting the tone of their organizations. By the very nature of the roles that they occupy, leaders are a fruitful source of organizational stories. They may be portrayed as heroes or villains, champions and winners or aloof losers, good guys or bad. Such stories have a tendency to become exaggerated and to develop into the myths that become absorbed deep within the organization's culture.

Stories such as those provided by scenarios of possible futures
when well told can also enter the repertoire of stories and myths
operating within your organization, offering a valuable context
(memories of the future) within which you, your managers and
others can discuss a wide range of possible story outcomes,
alongside your own strategies and plans. These discussions serve
to bring the story lines into the realm of the familiar so that,
when and if events occur that signal that something a little like
the events in a scenario story is starting to happen in reality, you
and those who have discussed them, will be sensitive to such
signals and be more likely to notice their possible implications.
Then, instead of ignoring them or fitting them into the comfortable categories of the familiar and the expected, you can begin to
anticipate their likely outcomes and take appropriate action.

The aim of scenario planning is not to attempt to generate an accurate prediction of the future. Such attempts miss the point and are
likely to be a tunnel-visioned extrapolation from existing views
and expectations and as such are doomed to failure.

It is important to recognize that as well as talking about creating
memories of the future in the plural, Arie de Geus also argues
that a number of quite different scenarios should be prepared –
no less than two and never an odd number, if those discussing
them are not to seek out the one in the middle as being "the most
likely" to anticipate the "real" future.

In Shell International, the scenarios were tested and quanti-
fied, run through sophisticated computer simulations in order
to check the consistency of the elements of each scenario and
of the data upon which it depended, and then captured as a
story written by a skilled storyteller. Organizations are full of
stories recounted in and after meetings, over coffee and lunch,
after hours and with families and friends. Stories such as those
provided by the skilled scenario writer find their way into the
organizational blood stream by similar routes.

> the end result is a series of consistent, plausible futures,
> which don't merely provoke thought [and debate]. If they're
> successful, they should provoke surprise and even emotion.
> "I never realized this could happen to us.[9]

You will be unlikely to have access to the resources of a Shell International to put behind the preparation and analysis of your organization's "memories of the future." But the principle of involving many different people in discussing a variety of memorable stories about possible futures for the business is one that all leaders would do well to note. Such stories alert us to warning signs and help us to make links to the lessons learned from previous experiences of the unexpected.

In his book, Storytelling in Organizations, Yiannis Gabriel writes:

> If organizations are jungles of information stories come to the rescue of meaning. Stories re-enchant the disenchanted, introducing wit and invention, laughter and tears into the information iron cage.[10]

Wide discussion of well-told scenario stories should be disturbing. They should ruffle feathers and take people out of the narrow focus that is the product of routine and a perspective born of concentrating on the successful delivery of targets and away from focusing on narrowly defined visions of success. The good scenario story causes people to stop and think, becoming sensitized to look out for the weak signals that can presage unexpected events that may, if not managed well, render such targets irrelevant.

4.8 How you respond to today's unexpected event can help prepare you for tomorrow's

Things appear to be going well. Revenues are looking good and your last presentation to the board earned you a round of applause. You have enjoyed the theater and are having dinner with your partner and a few friends when a mobile rings. It is yours.

You answer the phone and the operations director informs you that a major fire has broken out at the North London factory. The fire brigade and the salvage corps are on site, as is the factory manager together with several members of his team. The fire fighters appear to have the blaze under control. It is not clear whether anyone has been injured (or worse) and too soon to assess how much damage has been done.

What do you do?

Something like this happened to Graham. Whether what he did was the "right thing" or not isn't the point, we shall tell the story anyway.

4.6   Fire! Fire!

Having received just such a call when out to dinner one Sunday evening, Graham made his excuses and left. Fortunately, as he was planning to drive home, he had not been drinking. He drove quickly to the scene of the fire which was now cordoned off by the police. He made his way towards the police officer holding back the crowd and asked to be let through the barrier as he was a director of the company. Having so identified himself, he was taken to the incident control room where he was asked to explain how he had come to know that the building was ablaze and whether the company was experiencing any financial problems!

Lesson number one: he should have contacted the Police and let them know he was coming.

He quickly discovered that there was nothing that he could do about the fire and that the situation was in the hands of the experts. However, he did meet a number of junior employees who happened to live locally. In conversation with them and from the questions that they asked, he began to formulate the beginnings of a plan for what should happen when the professionals left the scene.

The following day these early plans needed to be modified but were extremely helpful in helping Graham and his director colleagues to minimize the disruption caused by the fire.

Lesson number two: Your presence may be valuable but don't get in the way of the experts.

Lesson number three: Reviewing and reflecting on the possible outcomes from an unexpected event needs to start

> immediately – and to involve those who are closest to the event and its likely consequences – before the facts give way to the myths and stories that will develop around it and begin to obscure them.

In the following chapter we explore in some detail the benefits to be gained from previewing, responding to, reflecting on and reviewing the unexpected. But first we need to summarize and to ask you some more questions.

4.9   Groundwork in summary

The groundwork that is necessary to prepare you for successfully managing the unexpected involves you first of all in knowing who you really are. This involves you in making sure that you are in touch with the values and beliefs that you hold, the touchstones that determine the boundaries that you are not prepared cross or to compromise. It requires that you be the person that you already are rather than modeling yourself on someone else who you are not. Role models are helpful but you will only succeed in your own eyes if you maintain your personal integrity, through "singing your own song" or "plowing your own furrow" or whatever other metaphor makes sense to you. Pay attention to who you are rather than trying to be the personification of a personal hero or of your perception of others who hold roles similar to the one that you happen to occupy.

The groundwork also involves you in building and reinforcing your organization's integrity. You can begin to do this by ensuring that its policies and procedures are relevant, robust and current and that they are developed and updated as close to their point of application as possible. They need to be aligned to the organization's purpose and goals, its strategies and plans, objectives and projects as well as to conform to more general standards and regulatory controls. They need to be meaningful within their wider organizational context and to be fit for purpose at their point of application, if they are to be seen as involving everyone while not stifling their initiative, creativity and capacity for innovation.

You need to find ways that can assist you and the people in your organization to keep in touch with what is going on in the outside world. You cannot afford to lose sight of its wider and ever shifting, political, social, economic, market and contexts. You need to be in a position to be able to contribute to the generation of "memories of the future" that will help to sensitize your organization to the weak signals that can alert it to the unexpected.

You can help yourself and your organization to anticipate the unexpected through making a point of looking out for, listening, observing and noticing such signals and, while driving for success, always being alert to the possibility of failure. You also need to encourage everyone else in the organization to do the same.

If you value your personal well-being, you should recognize the need to develop the "proper selfishness" that is necessary to remind you every now and then that you are a human being who is in a great many relationships with other human beings in every aspect of your life and not just an isolated leader of your organization.

4.10   More questions

- How clearly aware would you say you are of the values, attitudes and beliefs that may be guiding your actions?
- What stories and myths circulate about you in the organization?
- How do you learn about such stories and myths?
- Can you identify the fixed points, the touchstones that mark the boundaries that you would never cross?
- How often do you brush up against such touchstones?
- How frequently do you find that you are taken by surprise by the things that happen in your organization?

In your organization:

- Do people readily admit their mistakes so that they and others may learn from them?
- Do people expect to be "punished" for the mistakes that they make or hide them and cover them up?

- When things go wrong do people tend to ask what went wrong or who fouled up?
- Do people question, seek clarification or challenge proposals and processes for dealing with problems?
- Do your policies and procedures permit discretion to those at the coalface to take action to resolve problems and rectify mistakes?
- Are policies and procedures regularly updated and reviewed to ensure that they are relevant and current?
- When things go wrong are they escalated for resolution at a level higher up the organization?
- How easy do people find it to seek help?
- When something goes wrong how soon and how widely is the information about what has happened shared?
- When something goes wrong how accessible are those with the authority to put it right?
- How often do you and your colleagues check your assumptions?
- In general terms, how complex and interdependent are the processes upon which the organization depends?
- Would you say they were tightly coupled or loosely coupled?
- How much slack is there in the system – that can be taken up when something unexpected happens?
- How well do people listen to one another?
- What "memories of the future" exist within your organization?
- How widely are they shared?
- How do you think other people in your organization might answer these questions?

Understanding context – inside the organization: Obligations, values and managing paradox

5.1 Formal and informal leadership obligations

At the beginning of this book we asserted that leading an organization, whether as its CEO, managing or divisional director or general manager, whatever the particular leadership label you happen to bear, carries with it a number of obligations. Some of these will be set out in your letter of appointment, your service contract or laid down as the statutory responsibilities of anyone taking on the role of a director of a limited company. We believe that there are others, less formal, but just as important.

Of the obligations of this type, four appear to us to be quite fundamental. Though they are often assumed, they are frequently ignored or, if not ignored, they are often neglected, with negative consequences both for the leader and for the organization.

These obligations are:

1. As we have stated several times and will continue to emphasize, as an organizational leader you are obliged to be both conscious and continually aware of the tone that you set for the organization. You have no choice in this, since everything that you do, both formally and informally, when in role and

away from it and in your private life, contributes to what may be called the character of the organization that you lead – the way in which it is perceived by people both within and beyond its boundaries.

2. You are obliged to shape your organization's future through building and articulating a vision of what that future might look like and by providing a clear sense of the direction in which that future lies. This needs to be expressed in simple terms, terms to which everyone in the organization can relate personally.

3. You have an obligation to understand and to remain in touch with your organization's context – the wider social, economic, political and technological environment within which your business or organization functions, being sensitive to the constant change to which each of these contextual aspects is subject.

4. You have an obligation to develop and build the commitment of your organization's stakeholders to making that future become a reality. This involves you in developing your sensitivity to the differing needs of a variety of stakeholders both within and outside your organization. These stakeholders have needs that differ considerably from one another and which tend to be communicated in a variety of different "languages."

We explored the obligation to set the tone of the organization in Chapter 3. In this and the following two chapters we shall explore the other obligations and their implications in greater depth, together with the sometimes-paradoxical relationships that may exist between them.

In Chapter 6 we turn our attention to the need to marshal the resources that will enable you to build and maintain the enthusiasm and commitment of the people within your organization upon whom your success will depend.

Successfully delivering against these obligations is sometimes described as to be behaving in a "professional" manner. But what precisely does this mean?

5.2   The visible professional

To be "professional", implies working to a set of standards of knowledge and behavior that are clearly defined and acknowledged. It is the definition and the acknowledgement that are important. We turned to the Concise Oxford Dictionary for help. It defines a professional as someone who is "of belonging to, connected with, a profession", "performing for monetary reward", "a professional person".

This didn't help us very much.

Looking at the word, "profession" in the same dictionary took us a bit closer to what we have in mind, where the second dictionary definition of this word refers to a:

> "Vocation or calling esp. one that involves some branch of advanced learning or science"

We believe that the idea of a vocation or calling toward "leading and managing professionally" is key here and that this is closely coupled to the possession of a passion for continuous learning and challenge that is gained in the real world, hurly burly, rough and tumble that is the nature of contemporary organizational life. We are also talking about the attitude and approach that characterize the true professional, rather than one who is merely professionally qualified – for example, as a chartered member of the Institute of Directors, a chartered accountant or a Fellow of the Chartered Institute of Personnel and Development. Valuable as such qualifications may be, they do not guarantee a professionalism of approach to the management of a particular organization, with its own, unique group of employees, working together within a specific context and at one particular point in their organization's history.

It is what organizational leaders are, what they believe in and what they do that marks them out as being professional or not. It isn't simply a matter of what they know as evidenced by the qualifications that they hold.

Certainly, in-depth exposure to and familiarity with a general body of knowledge is necessary and will always be helpful to a director when taking leadership responsibility within an organization. But in our view, it is the development of patterns of appropriate behavior through continuous personal inquiry and learning, gained through a deep understanding of the organization in its particular context, that is the distinguishing mark of a truly professional approach to the practice of organizational leadership, rather than the possession of professional qualification.

Such understanding goes on to inform and guide the behaviors of those professional and insightful individuals who are the genuinely great leaders of organizations. Such people know, really know, their business, their people, their customers and other stakeholders in the wider context within which they are operating.

5.3   Shaping the future: values

The second obligation of the newly appointed leader of an organization is to give shape to the organization's future. Our experience suggests that to be able to do this, first requires that you have the unusually high level of self-insight, self-awareness and self-knowledge that we have just mentioned. These need to be firmly anchored in reality and untarnished by the blandishments and plaudits that you will receive from those wishing to curry your favor. While some of their expressed approval may be quite genuine, it may also be colored by their feeling that their future depends upon their ability to ensure that you think well of them.

In a nutshell, it means knowing who you are and then taking care not to fall into the fatal trap of believing your own bullshit! If you think that you might be at risk of suffering from this delusion, we suggest that you revisit the obstacle course that we described in Chapter 2.

You have to believe in yourself (if you don't why would anyone else?) but, at the same time, you must never fall victim to believing in your own myths. It is easy, in the interests of action and delivery, to lose touch with or to compromise your underlying values, attitudes and beliefs perhaps unwittingly. But it is a great deal easier to do so if you haven't taken the time to reflect on them regularly and then tested your recent behaviors against them, being careful to distinguish between those values and beliefs that you genuinely hold and those to which you aspire.

By values we mean those personal benchmarks or touchstones that define the boundaries making you the unique person you are; that distinguish those things that are acceptable to you from those things that are not. Values are the beliefs and ideas that you hold that transcend specific situations, opportunities, problems and crises. They determine the ways in which you respond to other people, to their behavior and to the unexpected events in which you will become embroiled. They are hierarchical, in that some are likely to be more strongly held than others but, together, they form a set of personal priorities that are systemically related. The values that you hold stimulate you to summon up the reserves of energy and emotion that you will require in order to fight for what you believe in.

Ultimately it is your values that make you who you are.

Many guides to effective leadership start by emphasizing the need to articulate your vision for the organization that you lead. We argue that before doing so you need to be sure that you really know yourself and what any vision that you hold or might develop really means to you. This requires you to know and understand your values.

Your values are by no means invulnerable or immutable. In London, back in 1961, the late Lindsay Anderson produced The Arsonists, a play written by the Swiss playwright, Max Frisch in 1953. The play demonstrates how it is possible to be persuaded, little by little, to perform acts that run totally counter to one's basic values and beliefs. The plot concerns a perfectly ordinary man who invites two strangers, both arsonists, into his house. Over the course of the play, he allows himself to be persuaded of the desirability of setting fire to his own home. Eventually, he does so.

The play is described as a work of absurdism but, as is often the case, it makes the valid point that, over time and in the absence of a willingness or opportunity to reflect, we may be induced or persuaded to do things that run totally counter to our self interest – and to those of the things we hold most dear. This is much more likely to happen if we haven't taken the trouble to understand and articulate our values to ourselves in the first place.

We also need to be aware that one person's values are another's prejudices. Unless they are held up and critically examined in the cold, harsh light of reality, they may lead us into all kinds of trouble. Our values filter the ways that we perceive both ourselves and other people. They can be powerful generators of self-fulfilling prophecies, allowing in evidence that supports and reinforces them and filtering out any evidence to the contrary. In order to prevent this tendency toward self-confirmation you need to bring your underlying values to the forefront of your consciousness and then subject them to an unflinching scrutiny.

You may discover that some of your values have degenerated into prejudices about yourself and about others. This is likely to lead you to define the world as you would like it to be rather than as it is reducing your capacity to respond appropriately to uncertainty and unexpected events. The popular British business psychologist, Peter Honey, has designed a range of exercises to help you to bring your values to the surface of your consciousness.[1] We have adapted the following three-step process from Honey's work.

5.1 Identifying your values

Step One:
Write down a list of statements about the values and beliefs that you hold about the ways in which people ought to behave (it doesn't have to be this particular set of values, but it is quite a good way to get started)

Step Two:

Share the list with someone close to you, whom you respect and trust, asking them which they recognize as being "you" and those which come as a surprise to them.

Step Three:

Modify the statements as you now think necessary, deleting those which you would *like* to be true about you or those that you believe you *ought* to hold. You can save these if you wish as things to which you may aspire, but don't kid yourself that these are values to which you are currently deeply attached.

© Peter Honey Publications Limited

Honey goes on to suggest that your values, attitudes and beliefs are largely interdependent and that, in combination, they exercise a powerful influence over what you do, how you behave and how you are seen by others. He argues that, once you are truly aware of your values, you will be in a position to modify them if you so wish.

We have an issue with the phrase "if you so wish." While we agree that this may well be possible in theory, our experience suggests that for the majority of us, changing our values is rather unlikely, at least in the absence of considerable effort, support and above all motivation. This is because we tend to hang on to those things that we feel have served us well, even when they may not have done so. If it was easy to modify our values, attitudes and beliefs, we don't believe that the profession of cognitive behavioral therapy would be expanding quite as rapidly as it is. The point is that we have held them unquestioned for so long that most of us tend to take our values for granted, becoming fully aware of them only when they are being threatened. We don't necessarily make our best decisions when we feel threatened.

Your values shape or constrain both your behavior and your decisions.

5.2　Credit crunch values

Dick Fuld, the CEO at Lehman Brothers when it collapsed, was known for the aggressive style that had earned him the nick name, "The Gorilla." He clearly enjoyed this image since he kept a stuffed gorilla seated in a chair in his office. He appeared to revel in the use of wild and aggressive imagery in the language he employed when in dictating how he expected people to behave.

Writing in the Sunday Times of 12 December, 2008, Andrew Gowers stated that Fuld had been *"the textbook example of the command and control CEO. More than that, to many employees and the outside world he was Lehman Brothers, his character inextricably intertwined with the firm's."*

Describing the climate that existed within the organization, one executive observed that it was very exciting, "you know, where we shoot our wounded and eat our young!"

The point we wish to emphasize here is that while Fuld's peculiarly aggressive style may have been unusual, even within the financial services sector, the style of its leader being "inextricably intertwined" with that of the firm is the norm.

Our question here, then, is how clear are you about what your values really are? Are you able to distinguish between what it is that is true about you as opposed to what you would like to be true about you? Can you spot the difference between the two?

If, when you have begun to identify the underlying values that shape who you are and what you do, you find that you are uncomfortable with what you see and wish to modify it, that is a different issue and one that is not the subject of this book. It is, however, the subject of a great many others!

In summary, then, our values are things that we acquire and develop over the course of many years. They have a tendency to become self-reinforcing as we filter out things that we observe which might cause us to challenge them and filter in those things that act to confirm them. Values can decay into prejudices that prevent us from becoming as effective as we might be. On the other hand, they can be eroded over time, leading us to behave in ways that we would have thought most unlikely or even impossible, such as tolerating unacceptable behavior, turning a blind eye to a misstatement of our company's profitability levels or even to burning down our own home.

We need to bring our values to the surface from time to time in order to scrutinize them in the light of reality, identifying those that we have outgrown (after all we didn't get eaten by the bears when we walked on the cracks in the pavement) or those that have now decayed and become prejudices. This can be an uncomfortable process and it may help you to share the experience of scrutinizing your values with a trusted friend or mentor.

If you leave putting your values to the test until you experience an unexpected opportunity or crisis, then it is more likely that you will find yourself taken by surprise. The responses that you make may be at odds with the values that you have professed to hold, letting you down. Your responses may prevent you from taking appropriate action or cause you to compromise that which you truly believe, diminishing yourself, in your own eyes, in those of your colleagues and of the employees upon whom your success depends.

5.3   Values 1

In March 1978 the super tanker, Amoco Cadiz, lost its steering gear off the coast of Brittany while carrying a cargo of oil owned by Shell. The value of the cargo considerably outweighed (by a factor of five) that of the vessel that was carrying it. In these circumstances it was not surprising perhaps that the owners of the vessel and those of its cargo had different priorities in coming to a decision as to what action should be taken to save the vessel and its cargo.

The ship's owners, based in Chicago, quickly sent two lawyers and a PR specialist to Europe to minimize the damage to the company's interests and reputation. On 24 March, while the lawyers were arguing their respective cases, violent seas caused the tanker to split in two. In total some 220,000 tons of oil escaped into the sea, creating a slick 18 miles wide and 80 miles long, polluting some 200 miles of the Brittany coastline. At this stage the Chicago based company sent an environmental specialist to advise on the clean up operation.

Sometime later the name of each of the company's fleet of tankers was changed, removing the word Amoco from each vessel.

Here is another, smaller-scale illustration.

5.4 Values 2

A service engineer working for a computer company was called to a customer site where the main server had "gone down." The engineer diagnosed a hardware fault and began to remove the server's casing. As he did so he slipped, putting his hand out to save himself which caused him to be badly burned as an electrical contact was made between two terminals.

The engineer was unable to return to work and submitted a claim to his employer for compensation for his injuries and for his loss of earnings. His claim was based on the allegation that the employer had been negligent in permitting the terminals beneath the server casing to be exposed. On the advice of its insurers, the employer countered the claim by stating that the engineer had broken company rules in failing to disconnect the server before removing its casing.

The claim and counterclaim were addressed by the lawyers and insurance companies of both the company and the engineer's trade union. The case ran on for more than two years without resolution. The engineer and his family suffered significant financial problems and the company's managing director was minded to make him an ex gratia, without prejudice payment in order to alleviate his and his family's distress. However, the company's lawyers and insurers advised him that to do so would be equivalent to acknowledging that the company had been at fault. Therefore no payment was made until eventually a mutually acceptable settlement was reached, many months after the original event.

The company had acted quite properly according to law. However the case cost it a great deal in terms of employee motivation and goodwill since the engineer's situation was widely known within the company. Its employee relations were significantly soured.

When sometime later the company published a statement of its values which included an indication that its highly committed team of employees were its greatest asset, it received a somewhat cynical response from its employees. Its service engineers expressed a particularly jaundiced view of the statement of company values.

What might Amoco and the computer company have done differently?

What would you have done in similar circumstances?

Values are never a matter of expediency.

5.4   Shaping the future: visions and acts of faith

A great many business and management books put the possession of an overarching vision at the top of the requirements of great leadership. We too rate it as being critical – just as long as leaders are absolutely sure of what their own values are and, therefore, sure of the nature of their personal commitment to the vision that they profess.

This because the fulfillment of a vision is first and foremost a matter of belief rather than of analysis and logic. As a leader you have to believe in your vision for without your belief, all the technical analyses, knowledge and skills that you can apply in the cause of making it a reality will be a waste of time. Without belief, there is no commitment; without commitment there is no passion and without passion there is insufficient determination to overcome resistance or to deal with the unexpected events that will combine to derail your vision's achievement.

You need to believe in your vision and the capacity of those to whom you provide leadership to accomplish it. These people need to come to believe in your vision through your willingness to share it with them and through the example you set and the organizational tone that you inspire.

Jim Collins suggests that if you happen to be the newly appointed leader of an existing organization, it would be as well to check out whether or not that you have the right people on the organizational bus before you announce and share your vision to the world.[2] You may find that you have the right vision but the wrong people or that you are in the wrong place.

John tells the following story from his own experiences as a newly appointed director.

5.5 Values on the line

Urgent action was required because the company was losing market share. Considerable savings were necessary and it was suggested that some of the company's bright young R&D scientists and engineers would have to be "let go." John was deeply disturbed by this. However, his disturbance turned to anger when he learned that, before his arrival on the scene, the company had entered into an agreement with the union representing the plant operatives and drivers of its distribution vehicles which over time became very costly. Under the terms of this agreement, productivity was low and costs were high, the company's vehicles often passed each other on the road, one full, the other half-empty. The fully loaded vehicle could well have been delivering half a load to the same location or one close to it from which the half loaded vehicle was driving away. Not only that, the shop stewards would not agree to any changes that would have improved customer service even though operatives and drivers were being paid at premium rates for low output.

John felt that this was immoral. The company was losing business, high contributing and highly qualified staff members were being threatened with lay off while the operatives and drivers were being paid large sums of money in return for low productivity and an inflexible attitude. John was advised that there was little or nothing that could be done about it because of the agreement that the company had previously entered into with the union. In his mind this was not only immoral it was also absurd since if these practices were allowed to continue, the company would go bust and everyone would lose their jobs.

John decided that he simply could not allow the situation to continue. To do so would have run totally counter to his own values. By allowing things to go on as they were not only would the company face ruin but he would be colluding in something in which he did not believe. His vision was a bleak one, Not all his board colleagues were supportive, feeling that a confrontation with the operatives and the drivers would be likely to provoke industrial action on a scale that would be crippling to the company. But John believed passionately that things could not be allowed to go on as they were and so he decided to take on the drivers, the operatives and their union.

The details do not concern us here. In summary, John explained the position and its implications to a few key managers. They were equally appalled. The agreement was cancelled, the operation reorganized and a new much more realistic deal was offered to the drivers to whom it was explained that the alternative was to look for another job. Although a number of John's fellow directors had anticipated Armageddon, there was in fact very little disruption; productivity was doubled and operating costs halved. The effectiveness of the vehicle fleet was greatly enhanced and the jobs of the R&D scientists and engineers were saved. John comments:

"I now understand that what my intuition and my sense of moral indignation were telling me was right. You have to believe it as well as knowing it and saying it. I was convinced that I had no choice. I could not be a director of a company that permitted such practices to continue. I believed that we had no choice because time was running out. I also believed that the actions we were taking were for the long term, that I would still believe that it was the right thing to do in ten years time – when I was retired."

If you wish to realize your visions and dreams you must believe in them sufficiently to enable you to make an act of faith when the situation demands.

5.5   Paradox and unreasonable truths

At the beginning of this chapter, we suggested that we become who we are as a consequence of modeling ourselves unconsciously on others, our families, our peers, heroes and leaders. Essentially, we are shaped by our experiences of other people's behavior in the contexts within which we interact with them. But increasingly things happen that make little or no sense within such contexts. We may discover that our heroes have feet of clay; that the values to which they encouraged us to adhere were only aspirations on their part; that they have changed their minds or behave in ways that run counter to the values that they claimed to espouse. Moreover, things occur beyond the boundaries of familiar contexts, requiring us to reappraise and possibly to redefine our situation and the relationship between ourselves and such contexts.

For example, broadband and the Internet have caused those engaged in broadcasting to conduct a fundamental reappraisal of the nature of their industry. Rather than programming for the mass of society, anticipating and providing for what it is believed that the members of that society want, broadcasters are being required to redefine their role in a society where masses of people are creating programs for themselves.

As an organizational leader you will constantly find yourself being challenged by unexpected events that conflict with what you have long accepted as reasonable, possible or true. Inevitably such paradoxical situations are very uncomfortable, having a tendency to provoke the response, "hang on a minute!" or, when the evidence is undeniable, "yes, but…" As an organizational leader, leading in conditions of uncertainty, you will need to become comfortable in situations where apparently self-contradictory statements are simultaneously true ("yes, and …" rather than "yes, but…").

For many years rational, empirical science has provided us with a sense of security. Quantum physics and other developments in such sciences now suggest that this sense of security has been unjustified. In organizations, a rational analytic approach towards managing has, we suggest, provided us with a comfort blanket similar to that provided in the past by the physics of traditional science. That blanket is beginning to show signs of being worn out and outmoded. When we are dealing with organizational decision-making we need to take into account issues such as "meaning", "power", "values" and "culture." Such matters are much less susceptible to logic and rational analysis The "facts" that we associate with such concepts are a great deal more subject to interpretation than are those associated with the laws of chemistry, the nature, gravity and minerals which have, themselves, been revealed to be full of contradictions and paradox. This leads us to suggest that leaders need to be able to live comfortably with conditions of such apparent contradiction and paradox of the kind listed in the examples with which we shall conclude this chapter.

As we shall discuss in the Chapter 6, the effective organizational leader develops a sense of shared ownership by successfully building a sense of commitment to a set of goals and values in all or at least most of its members. However, this sense of ownership and commitment tends to be enhanced the more the leader "gives it away." People who take on the challenge of greater responsibility are in a better position to experiment, to take risks and to question. Effective organizational leaders add value by encouraging this process to be widely shared even though taking place within clearly understood boundaries, rather than by restricting the burden of questioning and challenging to themselves. Thus the effective leader increases his or her authority the more that he or she gives it away while recognizing that at the end of the day, s/he is still accountable.

Thus, it is perhaps an uncomfortable truth that if you wish to be secure, you must be prepared to be challenged.

Here are a few more examples of the kinds of paradox with which you will need to be comfortable if you wish to become an effective leader of your organization:

5.6   Recurrent paradox

Recognise that everyone makes mistakes – including you. Encourage people to acknowledge errors by rewarding them when they admit to them. Then they and others can learn from them and, hopefully, avoid them in future – rather than cover them up or deny them.

Show zero tolerance for the kinds of ill discipline that leads to ladders being left unsecured – while encouraging a climate in which solution seeking is favored over assigning blame

Display conviction and confidence – while, at the same time, acknowledging uncertainty and the inevitability of the unexpected,

Recognize that "the devil is in the detail" – but keep your eye on the "bigger picture."

Specify boundaries that are clear enough to identify the responsibilities of business units, functions and projects – while being sufficiently "fuzzy" to cope with the unexpected. Always stay in touch with context if you wish to make sense of the unexpected when it happens.

Make time for reflection – but always be ready for action.

Develop the sense of being on the winning team throughout your organisation – but avoid making people feel like losers.

Always drive for change, innovation and improvement – but don't forget that tomorrow's success is dependent on today's business as usual.

5.6   Some more questions

- How well do you think you know the impact that your presence has on the organization and its culture?
- How would you describe the "tone" of the organization that you are leading?
- How do you think these groups of other people might describe the "tone" of your organization?
  - Your colleagues?
  - A group of recently recruited junior employees?
  - Your customers?
  - Your competitors?
- What actions are you taking to manage your own impact upon the organization and its "tone"?
- How would you describe the context within which your organization is currently operating?
- How do/might you communicate this perception to others?
- How well can you articulate the values that determine the way that you lead your organization?

- How do you ensure that that your actions and behaviors are in alignment with your values?
- How do you deal with inconsistencies between your actions and your values?
- How do you measure commitment in your organization?
- How do you demonstrate trust in those around you?
- How do you demonstrate that those around you can trust you?
- How do people around you know that you are listening?
- What processes have you/might you set up to test the level of consistency between organizational values and behaviors, quality of communications and feedback, willingness to question and challenge, levels of commitment?
- How do/might others respond to such testing?
- How do/will you manage their responses?

CHAPTER 6

Marshalling resources – building and managing commitment

6.1 Different ways of thinking: engagement and commitment

In this chapter we discuss two contrasting ways of thinking. Business leaders need to employ these in a balanced way when developing the goals that they wish their organizations to pursue and as they seek to gain the commitment of those upon whom they will depend if those goals are to become reality. The first of these modes of thinking owes much to the contribution that science, engineering and technology have made to the success of industrial societies over the past 250 years or so. This mode tends to be formally structured, emphasizes and favors the logical, the analytical and the objective and is popularly termed "left Brain" thinking.

The second mode of thinking is very different. It puts more emphasis on the imagination, the creativity, the flair and passion that the organizational leader needs to demonstrate and encourage others to share on the road to success. This mode favors the imaginative, the emotional, the tacit, the subjective and the meaningful and has been called "right Brain" thinking.

The "left brain, right brain" metaphor should not be taken literally since the two modes of thinking are not, of course, mutually exclusive. Each may contribute to the effectiveness of the other. However, we do suggest that these different modes of thought may give rise to two quite different kinds of organizational language that can significantly inhibit performance, if they are not joined together through the application of a third mode of thinking that successfully integrates both rational-analytic and imaginative-emotional modes of thought and language.

We suggest that failure to link these two forms of language originates with a tendency to become overdependent on one or other of the two modes of thinking arising from reluctance or from an inability to recognize and integrate them effectively. Thus while erring in favor of the rational-analytic mode may be appropriate to the operation of a highly structured, highly stable, process-driven business or government bureaucracy, while favoring the passionate, emotion-based commitment may be needed in the start-up phase of an entrepreneur-led media company, a balance between the two is essential over the longer-term and especially when dealing with unexpected events.

Integrating these thought processes and the languages that are associated with them is, we suggest, a key requirement to understanding your business and communicating effectively with, its people and its stakeholders and to ensuring that you have their on-going support and commitment.

6.2   Rational-analytical thinking

Many leaders of large-scale businesses and public-sector organizations, together with their managers and advisors appear to be in thrall to the contributions that rational-analytical thought processes have made to the technological and economic achievements of the last 250 years. This is hardly surprising since such thinking as it has been applied within the fields of pure and applied science and engineering has provided us with the steel works, the oil refineries, the transportation systems, the silicon chips and the information and communication networks upon which our twenty-first century society depends.

The contribution of science and technology to past economic success has led to a perception of the role of the manager as being one that also requires a formal, structured approach to addressing the challenges of organizing and managing – an approach that treats them as though such challenges are just like those of science and engineering. In other words, such challenges or problems have come to be regarded as ones that may be solved through the application of the appropriate tools, techniques and approaches in the "correct" manner in order to generate the "right" solutions. But this is the same as treating a problem as though it were a puzzle to which the correct answer exists, somewhere "out there", if only we can find it through the rigorous application of the "right" analytical method of problem solving. From this it follows that, if problems of organization and management are susceptible to rational-analytic problem solving methods (the methods of scientific management from the 1930s to the 1950s or of management science from the 1950s to the 1980s), then the language that is employed to communicate these problems and their solutions also needs to be formalized – as is that of scientific method. In other words, it needs to be a language that while complex, is unambiguous, objective, impersonal and formal. Such language, however, has also provided us with the highly sophisticated, formulae driven, securitized financial instruments that lie at the core of the credit crunch of 2007 and 2008 – a language so complex that it appears to have been beyond the comprehension of the leaders of the organizations that marketed such instruments.

When we were starting out on our management careers, the emphasis on the business courses that we attended and in the management books that we read was upon leading, planning, organizing, delegating and controlling. Our job, we were told, was to be effective in each these areas in order to deliver the output requirements of the roles that we occupied. According to one management guru of the times, Bill Reddin,[1] to be effective in delivering the output requirements of our management roles was, indeed, our only job. The books that we read had titles such as The Principles and Practice of Management, Decision and Control and Systems of Organization[2] and they provided us with considerable comfort and encouragement by suggesting, though perhaps not quite in so many words, that there is indeed a body of knowledge "out there", which we might acquire if we were sufficiently diligent and scientific in our approach towards the gathering of facts (data) and in subjecting them to rigorous and objective analysis. The application of such methods would enable us to discharge our managerial responsibilities for planning, organizing, delegating and controlling appropriately and thus meet Reddin's dictum that our job, our only job, was to be effective.

A major benefit arising from this form of thinking and from the kind of language associated with it is that it is precise, it is focused and it helps to facilitate the establishment of "communities of practice"; groups of colleagues with a shared approach and a common language by means of which such groups can function.

A key tenet of the scientific method is the requirement for replicability. Before the results of an experiment may be said to have demonstrated an outcome that proves conclusively the hypothesis that it was designed to test, it must be shown to be capable of replication by others. The language of science reflects this and this language has been transferred to the formal language of management.

Such language has another facet, beneficial at first, in that it helps to distinguish those who have a facility with its terminology and nuances ("us") from those who do not ("them"). But this obviously has a number of downsides too, not least in that it begins to reduce "our" capacity to communicate effectively with "them".

As this approach to managerial thinking developed in different areas of organizational practice, each area has provided us with its own population of specialists and experts upon whom we have been able to call as their knowledge has grown and their language has become more esoteric. But each field of expertise has also developed its own set of principles, disciplines, traditions and variants of formal language, each of which is quite specific to their specialist community. In order to be able to converse meaningfully with such specialists, it has become necessary for each field to call upon integrating roles whose occupants know sufficient of the differing languages and terminologies to be able to establish those areas of common ground within which meaningful communication may take place.

The most important of all such integrating roles is that of an organization's leader.

By and large, this common ground has come to be represented as the formal, rational and logical management language of the plans, reports, agenda, proposals and memoranda that all of us encounter daily. Such language is currently going through another metamorphosis as more and more organizational communication takes place via email, with its own protocols, etiquette and acronyms.

However, formal language that is a derivative of rational-analytical thinking, in whatever form, is quite different from the informal, day-to-day language by means of which we get things done.

As the years have gone by, experience has taught us that, helpful though formal language has been, it has severe limitations. It does not provide us with sufficient breadth of meaning and subtlety to enable us to engage and deal with the wide range of challenges with which we are confronted. These challenges impact us personally as well as in our work roles, not least because much of the elusive body of knowledge related to such challenges remains doggedly beyond our reach, "out there" and, therefore, a source of frustration and irritation to us.

Moreover, we have come to appreciate that there are other bodies of knowledge (that to us also are "out there") of which we need to have at least a passing understanding in addition to that which relates to our own particular area of responsibility and which is the common parlance of our own particular community of practice. For the two authors, this has required us, for example, to develop a degree of familiarity with specialist disciplines other than our own, such as, finance, marketing, human resource and risk management.

6.1 The operations director's nightmare

On one occasion, when Graham was acting as consultant to a large logistics and distribution company he found himself in a meeting where the company's IT specialists were presenting their proposals for a new market-intelligence system to its top management team. The IT people had obviously done a great deal of work on the system and were very proud of the potential benefits that they believed it would bring to the business.

Some way into their presentation, Graham noticed that the operations director had stopped doodling on his pad and was busily keying emails into his BlackBerry, obviously paying very little, if any, attention to the presentation. Graham looked around the room and concluded that at least half of those present were not engaged with the presentation. At that point he appreciated that he was not listening either!

Although the presenter was following most of the rules of effective presentation, emphasizing benefits rather than features, keeping the content of his PowerPoint images to a minimum, etc., the language that he was using excluded the majority of those in the room, being full of I.T. jargon little of which was directly relevant, let alone meaningful, to the marketing specialists and those present from disciplines other than IT.

At the end of the presentation the managing director responded, politely thanking the IT team for its presentation and advising them that he and his colleagues would discuss what they heard and "get back" to them (how often that last phrase turns out to be the kiss of death!).

Over coffee Graham buttonholed the operations director and asked him what he had thought of the presentation. By way of an answer the director responded, "Do you know, I have a recurrent nightmare in which I am visited by the IT director, the finance director and the marketing director. All of them

> are offering to help me and each of them has brought his lawyer. They are all talking at once and I don't understand a single word that anybody is saying. Ten minutes into that guy's presentation I felt the nightmare coming on."

As our lives as directors and managers of organizations become more complicated, so the number and availability of resources to assist us to come to grips with new areas of knowledge and skill also increase. We have access to consultants who can assist us, for example, in the application of business process reengineering, specialists in SAP, Six Sigma and the Balanced Scorecard and have been helped to identify our core competencies as we have gone about rightsizing our businesses.

All of this suggests that the body of knowledge concerned with the best in management practice and which can help provide the solutions to most of the problems that we encounter is growing exponentially. Taking in even a small proportion of all this additional knowledge and information would not have been possible without the benefits that have arisen from the developments in information and communications technology of recent years. We work from virtual offices and in virtual teams facilitated by Bluetooth enabled email networks that we are able to access and interrogate via our laptops, mobile phones and PDAs. In so doing we process volumes of information so large as to have been inconceivable as recently as the late 1990s.

Notwithstanding all these developments, however, the sneaking suspicion still remains that much critical knowledge still remains "out there" and elusive when we need it, causing us to experience the familiar paradox that comes from realizing that the more we know, the more we know we need to know.

This can generate a great deal of anxiety, not least at senior levels in organization where those in positions of leadership and authority may come to feel increasingly that while they are in command, they are very far from being in control. One would certainly hope that the heads of those banks that developed such incredibly sophisticated products, the complexity of which surpassed most human understanding and finally brought them to their knees during the second half of 2008 experienced at least some of this anxiety before they called upon governments to bail them out.

Such anxiety and related emotions are personal; they are deeply felt and cannot be communicated in the kind of formal language that is derived from thought processes that are primarily determined by rationality and formal analysis. Such language is standardized, impersonal and objective. As such it can be committed to reports, and presentations; it can be replicated and justified. But it can also be exclusive; a private language between experts that encourages others to disengage from the conversation. It can appear legalistic, bureaucratic and cold. It can be reductionist, functioning to close down rather than opening up discussion and debate as "non experts" feel themselves excluded, experiencing their own sense of loss of control.

As in the case of the IT specialist's presentation that we described above, there is a danger that the response to these feelings of exclusion and disengagement will simply be to "smile and salute" – to shrug and acquiesce in what is being proposed rather than giving it the total commitment or outright rejection that is required – an approach to problem solving that is best described as "fudging".

An altogether different style of thinking and a different kind of language is required to counter such feelings of exclusion and disengagement.

6.3   Imaginative-emotional thinking

To capture the interest and commitment of the operations director and his colleagues at the meeting that we just described, the IT specialist would have needed to engage each member of his audience at a personal and emotional level, one that appealed to their individual imaginations, allowing each one the possibility of joining him in his enthusiasm for his subject.

This would have required him to adopt a language that was quite different from the formal, rational and objective language of his area of specialist knowledge and competence. But he would not have needed to go so far as to employ the different, though still formal, language of each of the specialisms that were represented around the room, simply to use a language that engaged them personally and at the level of their emotions – a language that is characteristic of anecdotes and story-telling.

A key aspect of your role as a leader of your business requires that you deal with the unplanned consequences of the actions that you have planned. You are likely to find that in your leadership role, you will spend considerably more time in reacting, responding and engaging in a succession of dialogs and conversations with many people from different disciplines and at different organizational levels than you do in the more formal matters of planning, organizing etc.

The ways in which our own businesses moved forward seems to have been determined as much by the outcomes of these often "messy" and sometimes stilted conversations as they were by the more formal planning and managerial processes that were employed by the specialists and experts upon whose support these processes often depended. This is not to say that such processes were inadequate, only to indicate that they could communicate only part of the story. This may quite literally be the case because these formal processes do not set out to tell stories at all.

The formal language of plans, reports and proposals is quite different from that of the anecdotes, stories and myths which engage people's imagination and emotions.

This is the kind of a language with the capacity to engage the individual at a personal level. It is an informal language of anecdote, of metaphor and of play, the language of everyday conversation that grabs the listener as the unique individual that he or she is rather than as the performer of the specialist or professional roles that they happen to occupy.

Such language is informed by a very different mode of thinking.

Anecdotes are rich in metaphor and often seem to go off at tangents; to be fragmented and somewhat chaotic, but they help to convey meanings that colleagues and staff appreciate and understand and with which they can identify. Such language conveys something of ourselves, our character, our emotions and feelings. It is not primarily objective and rational–which is almost certainly one of the reasons that so much attention has been paid to efforts to remove it or screen it out of formal managerial communications.

To head a company, division or branch or indeed to lead any form of complex organization is to occupy a position at the conjunction of many different and often conflicting networks or organizational "power circuits". Many if not most of these networks are substantially overloaded with the consequence that, as the capacity of our organizations to process information has increased, so the ability of different interest-groups within the organization to communicate effectively with one another appears to have gone down.

6.4 Toolkits and snakepits

The authors of a recent academic management book, Developing Strategies for Change[3] offer us some clues. They suggest that modern management theories and techniques are located within a landscape of business and management that represents itself as a "complex network of mechanical instruments" that you can control, provided you have access to the right toolkits (SAP, Six Sigma, SWOT analysis, business process reengineering, stakeholder analysis, for example).

As we suggested earlier in this chapter, communication between members of the different interest-groups who inhabit this landscape, whether as colleagues, customers, staff or consultants, needs to be in terms that make sense within its "mechanistic" or formal context (i.e. our first, rational-analytical mode of thinking). Each "machine" in the network operates according to its own book of rules and maintenance manuals, which are "written" in the same logical, analytical language in terms of formal theories of management and professional practice.

Such language encourages, perhaps assumes, a belief that everyone involved within an organization knows and understands what it is all about, what its purpose is and that they are all more or less equally committed to the achievement of its goals. People by and large are assumed to be collaborative, so that most of the problems that arise are seen as ones that may be reduced to a kind that can be resolved by people who have acquired the necessary and relevant skills and who can apply the appropriate techniques which are essential to the provision of effective solutions.

However, the authors also suggest that this landscape is rarely the same as that of the "lived experiences"' of managers and others in organizations throughout the world. They claim that most people, far from regarding their organizations as well-oiled machines or sophisticated, carefully designed, rational systems, are much more likely to see them as "snake pits" in which, "everything is always falling apart, and [where] peoples' main activity is to ensure that it doesn't fall on them; no one really knows what is going on, though everyone cares about what is going on because there is danger in not knowing; anxiety and stress are constant companions and people take little pleasure in dealing with each other, doing so primarily for their own purposes or because they cannot avoid being so used themselves. Management problems are seen as intractable – survival is the name of the game."[4]

We believe that both these metaphors – the toolkit and the snakepit – capture some aspects of the experiences of some people in some organizations. They certainly reflect aspects of our own experiences and those of some of the directors and managers with whom we have worked. But the descriptions are, in the end, caricatures that do not capture anything approaching the reality of life as experienced within all organizations. The experiences of working in Apple or a Virgin company; in Ryanair, the British Post Office or the National Health Service are likely to be quite different from one another, while all demonstrating some characteristics of both the toolkit and the snakepit.

What the toolkit and snakepit metaphors do bring out is the great diversity of organizational experience. In particular, they demonstrate the extent of the communication challenge that is faced by leaders of organizations, if they are to enable members from different backgrounds, with different peer groups and different agendas and who attempt to communicate through their own esoteric professional languages, to understand one another and become united in their commitment to a set of common goals and objectives.

We also have plenty of experience to suggest that people often do behave and attempt to communicate with one another as though the rational/mechanical landscape is in fact the only one within which leadership is practiced. Similarly, we realize that interventions from the snake pit do occur but that they are often seen as aberrations, problems generated by people who are unwilling or unable to play by the rules of the formal management game. In fact the failure may not be a feature of the motives of such people as much as it is a failure of the respective languages of the toolkit and the snakepit to result in genuinely effective communication.

If managers are, in terms of Bill Reddin's dictum, to meet the output requirements of their jobs effectively, then they must rely to a great extent upon the formal, rational language upon which different disciplines and specialist groups depend. But their outputs must be integrated if the organization is to survive, let alone succeed. So this language needs to be mediated by a second, imaginative-emotional language that captures the attention of each individual at a personal level, building on their enthusiasms, providing them with a picture of a possible future with which they can engage and through which they can develop a sense of personal ownership.

This is the language of oratory, the kind of language employed by Barrack Obama in his election night, "Yes we can", speech in Chicago. It is the kind of language that needs to be employed to generate the enthusiastic engagement and commitment of colleagues, staff and employees across the organization in whatever discipline and at whatever level. As such it cannot be dismissed as the language of the snakepit. We clearly need both the language of the formal, mechanistic kind which is standardized and replicable and that in the style of oratory that engages people emotionally and meets their needs for communication that is meaningful to them at a personal level.

6.5　Integrated thinking

While you may not need the ability as an orator that has been demonstrated by the current occupant of the White House, it is your responsibility as leader of your organization to engage the imaginations and commitment of the people upon whom your success depends. This requires you to be able to integrate both modes of thinking and to bring together the kinds of language that is characteristic of them both.

To do this successfully you need to really know and understand:

- your business;
- your colleagues and your employees;
- your stakeholders:
  - your customers;
  - your suppliers;
  - your shareholders
  - and your competitors.

almost as well as you know yourself, your values and the passions and emotions which engage you and will engage others.

6.6　How well do you know your business?

To lead it professionally and successfully you need to know and understand your business in its broadest sense and within its wider context. This may appear to be a statement of the blindingly obvious, but we have observed many examples of situations in which organizational leaders have taken critical decisions that revealed little (or an extremely limited) understanding of what their business actually was or had the potential to become.

We have also seen examples of organizations where those at the top have come to appreciate that the business in which their company has been successful over many years has no long term future, requiring a fundamental re-appraisal of what it needs to be if it is going to survive.

Two examples spring to mind.

6.2 Rethinking the business 1

For many years a major brewing group provided the bench-mark for excellence for tradition and quality, both in its products and in the establishments (public houses and hotels) through which many, possibly most, of those products were sold. Two significant changes in the wider context within which the company was operating forced the group's top management to re-define its business. The first of these was a government decision that the long established link between the breweries and their "tied public houses" was anti-competitive and, therefore, to make such links illegal. The second was the opening up of the UK brewing market to competition from European breweries consistent with the terms of the European Union's single market policy. These two changes fundamentally altered the context within which the company was trading.

The chief executive asked himself just what business his company was now in and in what areas it possessed the significant capability that would ensure that it had a long-term future in the changed context within which it found itself. He concluded that the areas in which he and his colleagues needed to view their business were those of leisure and hospitality, which had previously been regarded as adjuncts to the core business rather than as the core itself.

According to this view, while still significant, what had been seen as the company's core business for many years, the brewing of high quality, premium English beers, had now become a second-order function.

The chief executive decided that he had a choice. He could persuade the board to take that function back to the company's core by pursuing an aggressive program of acquisitions of European and of other British breweries. Alternatively, he could argue that the board should raise the capital funding that would be required to finance the company's rapid expansion into a more broadly based hospitality and leisure business. It could achieve this by selling off most of its breweries – what had been its heart, its core business for several generations of directors, managers and employees.

The chief executive and his allies weighed the odds between the two options and concluded that the second would be the one most likely to succeed in the long term. Not surprisingly, they had something of a problem in selling their recommended solution to the board as a whole and then to convince the company's shareholders to support them. The decision really would mean abandoning the public image and traditions for which the company was famous and betting on the strength of its brand to carry it into entirely new markets, ventures and partnerships.

While it was possible to produce the statistics and rational analyses that indicated the strengths and weaknesses of both options, it was the imagination, passion and the belief of the chief executive that persuaded the board to undertake the act of faith to abandon its traditional core business and commit to the pursuit of the second option.

The decision paid off and the company went on to become a highly successful player in the global hospitality and leisure market, achieving levels of growth and profitability that could not have been imagined had it stuck with its traditional core brewing business, even assuming that it would have survived the acquisition wars that the restructuring of the market subsequently unleashed.

Part of being the professional leader that we described in the last chapter is the capacity to understand your business both as it is and as it might become, rather than allowing yourself to be persuaded that things are and should continue to be as they have always been. This requires you to be willing to be able to move right out of your comfort zone in order to contemplate difficult choices with regard to the future, when both colleagues and opponents are reluctant to do so. It requires you to be able to appreciate the analyses necessary to informing your choices and to communicate the reasons for exercising the particular choice that you make in a way that demonstrates your personal conviction, passion and enthusiasm for it so that others may join you equally enthusiastically.

Having made your choice you need the resolve to follow that choice through to its conclusion, in the full knowledge that the journey will be deeply disturbing to many and extremely uncomfortable for you. You must recognize that all such change is painful and acknowledge the impact of this as you push for it to happen.

A second example that illustrates this is provided by that of a fast moving, multinational consumer goods company.

6.3 Rethinking the business 2

The company had been globally successful in producing and marketing a widely diversified product range around the world. Its recently appointed chief executive was determined not to undermine the reputation that his company had established for expansion and growth, even though he recognized that the considerable costs of doing so were becoming highly visible on the company's balance sheet. This was starting to make both shareholders and the business media extremely nervous.

Sensing that alarm bells were about to ring, he developed a two-pronged strategy. The first of these involved continuing to pursue rapid diversification and growth, while the second involved removing several hundred millions of dollars of cost from the business, through a process of radical, business process reengineering.

He retained a merchant bank and a major firm of international management consultants to advise him. The consultants were charged with taking out the millions of dollars worth of cost from the company.

The consequences were little short of disastrous. The chief executive and his acquisition team were constantly on the lookout for new businesses to buy and did so at a rapid rate. Meanwhile the team of consultants assigned to remove costs from the company proved to be made up of highly qualified, highly ambitious young business school graduates. These young Turks were managed by senior consultants who were deeply ingrained in the consultancy practice's particular approach and were understandably jealous of its reputation. They also possessed considerable skill and in-depth knowledge of business process reengineering. But none of them had any great appreciation of the particular company, its people and its culture.

The consultancy team proceeded to develop the means for taking the required costs from the company's existing businesses, by streamlining its processes and by cutting jobs.

Unfortunately, the managers and specialists who were responsible for running these existing businesses became confused and somewhat fearful, since it soon became apparent that they themselves were quite likely to be the source of some of the costs that needed to be removed from the business.

Morale plummeted and, not surprisingly, some of the most talented managers began to jump ship – (a) because they felt threatened and (b) because they could easily find other jobs.

The company's share price started to tumble, while the integration of the newly acquired businesses proved to be extremely challenging to an increasingly confused and over-stretched management team. The chief executive circulated a memo to all staff announcing the introduction of a pro-gram of further cutbacks. The memo thanked the staff for their understanding and commitment and added that the company would emerge with a fitter, more agile and more competitive organization.

He did not specify that this would involve making some 15–20 percent of the workforce redundant. He probably didn't need to. The managers and staff had seen it coming anyway.

It seems to us that the chief executive was guilty of two cardinal sins. First, he managed to lose sight of the business that he was in, thereby causing his senior managers to become confused about it as well. Secondly, he lost touch with the people in his organization upon whom his own success depended. In so doing he lost their commitment and their loyalty.

Within a couple of years the company had merged with another conglomerate and its once household name had been consigned to history.

6.7   How well do you know your people?

If the first requirement of being professional as an organizational leader is to know, really know, your business, then the second is to know your people equally well, recognizing them as the complete individuals that they are rather than merely as the labels that their role positions place upon them.

When taking up your role at the top of an organization, you will be under considerable pressure to make things happen and to get things done. Part of this pressure stems from the expectations that you have of yourself and part from the expectations of those who have appointed you. But once you are in post, the expectations of those to whom you are required to provide leadership as head of the organization become just as important.

Throughout the 1980s it was often suggested that a "bias for action" was a sign of potential organizational excellence. But please bear in mind that every single action that you take as a leader will generate a reaction on the part of other people. This is why we see knowing and developing your understanding of the people upon whose responses your success is going to depend as being crucial. It will determine your ability to tune in to and to capture their enthusiasms so that they may become keen to commit to your goals.

6.4 Is everyone on board?

This was brought home very powerfully to us during an encounter with a remarkable woman who had just been appointed as the chief executive of a local authority that had been experiencing major problems for a considerable period. Its budgets were massively overspent; its council tax was under-collected; rubbish lay in its streets and a large proportion of the lighting for those streets had not worked for months, if not for years. Its management-staff relations were poor and the strategy of the authority's political leaders seemed to be one of blaming just about everybody other than themselves.

She told us that she proposed to work on the hypothesis that around 5 percent of those employed by the authority would back her to the hilt in bringing about the changes she thought were necessary. Another 10 percent or so might give her the benefit of the doubt and, therefore, be prepared to be biased in her favor. Around 65 percent would probably be largely indifferent to anything that she proposed or did, having seen other chief executives come and go with little or no positive change or improvement to show for their brief presence in the organization. She acknowledged this and accepted that one of the challenges that she faced was to demonstrate convincingly that her leadership would be different. She suspected that a further 15 percent were likely to be negative towards whatever proposals she might make.

Finally, she guessed that the remaining 5 percent of the people in the organization would be likely to be what she described as "saboteurs" who, for whatever motives, would actively seek to ensure that she failed, by any means that they could find.

Her strategy towards the different groups in the organization was as follows:

The 5 percent who would back her without question, she told us, needed to be provided with a degree of "gentle but firm managerial leadership" so that they did not make errors as a consequence of what might prove to be blind faith on their part.

The support of the 10 percent of people who were prepared to give her the benefit of the doubt needed to be acknowledged, encouraged and nurtured with a degree of gratitude.

She proposed to woo the 65 percent who were indifferent, by being positive, being visible, and by doing a great deal of listening to and communicating with them.

She planned to challenge the negative 15 percent by continually presenting and demonstrating to them the benefits that could arise for them from any changes that she proposed, with the objective of encouraging them to join the group of 65 percent who were, at least, indifferent.

But her first priority was to identify, confront and root out the final 5 percent who were saboteurs – and fire them. From this group she expected and would give no quarter.

It was likely, she said, that the authority would have to part company with people from all of the different groups that she had identified. She would do so, with fairness, with compassion, with openness and without pretense, acknowledging that this would be a painful process for all concerned.

We were struck by the fact that the chief executive had said that she expected that members of the saboteur group would be found at all levels in the organization. She guessed that those at the most senior levels would prove to be the most difficult to identify because they were likely to have perfected their skills of negativity over many years. If they remained in the organization, she said, they would poison its culture, sapping both its and her own energies, making it impossible for her to achieve the goals to which she had committed when she was appointed. We heard later that it had been agreed that a senior member of the executive board would be leaving.

Hers was a courageous approach and almost certainly a necessary one. It worked, for a while, but it took its toll on her and we learned that, after a couple of years, she had moved on.

We discussed this story, and concluded that, while we might argue with the details, we could certainly agree with the gist of her analysis. Among John's major regrets about his own role as a managing director was that he had not dealt with saboteurs sufficiently early enough. He had recognized that he had certainly had one or two among his fellow executive directors. Not confronting them head-on enabled them to distract him from his priorities and to divert his energy, simultaneously conveying the message "down the line" that not giving your full commitment could be regarded as being an acceptable position to take.

Graham recalls that one of the most frustrating aspects of his role as consultant and advisor to directors and chief executives was that so many of them were reluctant to engage in the difficult conversations that are involved in confronting those who were clearly undermining their ability to achieve their goals and objectives. They were often ready to accept the logic and analysis that told them that such conversations were necessary but then could not bring themselves to deal with the emotions that such conversations would involve.

The costs to you and to the business for which you are responsible, in terms of the energy that saboteurs will drain from you and in the ways that they can, if you let them, distract you from the issues that are crucial to your organization's future, far outweigh the discomfort and unpleasantness that you will experience in sniffing them out and getting rid of them. We fully understand that there will be a great deal of unpleasantness while you go through the process of identifying and removing saboteurs. But that is itself a measure of whether or not you mean business and whether you really mean what you say. If you are seen knowingly to allow those who are sabotaging your efforts to remain in your organization, why on earth should the 50 or 60 percent of employees, who are at best neutral towards you, sign up to join the ranks of your committed supporters, when they see you as tolerating those who are actively opposing you? If they don't sign up, then the saboteurs will have won.

But we fully recognize that such confrontation is a tough call.

Jim Collins[5] writes in his book (Good to Great) that, "getting the right people on the bus (and the wrong ones off the bus)" comes before determining precisely where your bus is going. He contrasts this position with that of those business leaders who take up the reins of a company and quickly announce their vision, strategy and reorganization plans. Only then do they seek out the people who will be needed to sign up to these plans.

The trouble with this approach, Collins suggests, is that it depends too much on the imaginative-emotional mode of thinking, becoming too personal, too strongly identified with the personality of the individual who happens to be leading the organization at one particular point in time. When he or she departs, he suggests, things are likely to fall apart, since loyalty and commitment have been developed to the unique vision of a particular person, rather than to one that was more widely shared. Far better to start by discovering what you have; to come to a clear understanding of the business that you are in and then to engage the commitment of as many of those who are already working in it as you possibly can, while rigorously weeding out those who will actively undermine you. It is, perhaps, significant that Collins uses the word "rigorous" rather than "ruthless". The latter term may sound fashionably "macho" but it seldom delivers the goods over the long haul. He suggests three, practical disciplines for being rigorous when making decisions about people in your organization. These are summarized below:

6.5 Taking people decisions

1. When in doubt, don't hire – keep looking. (Corollary: A company should limit its growth based on its ability to attract enough of the right people.)
2. When you know you need to make a people change, act. (Corollary: First be sure you don't simply have someone in the wrong seat.)
3. Put your best people on your biggest opportunities, not your biggest problems. (Corollary: If you sell off your problems, don't sell off your best people.)

Good to Great, Jim Collins (copyright © 2001)

We think that this is sound advice. You cannot deliver organizational success on your own. Making sure that you are supported
by people who are, at worst, neutral to your role in the achievement of such success has to make a great deal of sense.

6.8   How well do you know your stakeholders?

The next four areas:

- your customers;
- your suppliers;
- your shareholders
- and your competitors.

concern vital groups of stakeholders, people who will hurt if
you fail and, just as importantly, people who may hurt if you
succeed. You need to know and understand what it is that your
customers are buying from you and why it is that they are buying
from you rather than from the competition. You need to know
how the competition perceives you and anticipate its response to
your new initiatives.

This requires you to put yourself in your customers' shoes when
they ask themselves, for example: why, when we can get good
service from our online bookseller should we not get service of
the same quality from this supplier even though it is operating in
quite a different field?

Recognizing the importance of such questions may also cause
you to reassess just who your competitors are. While they will
almost certainly continue to include those that sell products
that compete with your own, they are also likely to include
those with whom your customers compare your company's
performance. This may have nothing whatsoever to do with
the quality of your product lines and services but everything
to do with whether they like and respect the manner in which
you supply them as compared with other companies with
which they do business – regardless of whether or not they

like you. This is not a matter of logic and rational analysis, but very much one of emotion and personal feeling. You need to work hard to ensure that such comparisons are nearly always favorable to you.

Such engagement may involve feelings of fun and happiness, sadness and grief, excitement and anxiety. It involves sensitivity and a willingness to be kind. Why is it, we wonder, that so many businesses announce redundancy programmes just before Christmas or the New Year holidays. Is it because the holidays happen to coincide with their financial year ends or because it enables their managements to recover from the personal impact of their difficult conversations over the break?

Shareholder value is a key driver of business priorities and the need to keep your shareholders, the City and the financial media happy has been a major demand on the time and resources of most company leaders. But as the main measure of a business' performance, shareholder value can become obsessively dangerous, leading to a concentration on too limited an indicator – one that may actually run counter to the long-term well-being of the business, as the following story illustrates.

6.6 Growth at all costs

The president of a multinational conglomerate was exceedingly proud of the fact that his company's profitability had grown, quarter by quarter for something approaching 40 successive quarters. Maintaining this track record, much admired on Wall Street, became a key driver for each of the CEOs of the businesses for which the president had overall responsibility. Unfortunately the inevitable market downturn, when it came, happened to coincide with a period of rapid technological innovation and market diversification. When the company should have been investing heavily in research and development in order to keep pace with the

competition, the president, with the support of an acquies-
cent group board, insisted that the company's track record
of quarter-by-quarter growth had to be maintained "at all
costs".

So the R&D and marketing budgets were cut. "All costs,"
turned out to include the company's being late to market
with new products and ultimately to its being acquired by
a smaller competitor within a couple of years of the president's unfortunate judgement.

6.9   Building commitment

When researching into the ways in which a number of directors
made sense of and learned from the change processes in which
they were engaged, it became clear to us that the task of building
commitment was one that, like managing the process of change
in one's business, is ongoing, endless and forever. One very successful CEO explained that this can be quite draining because, as
she explained, it involved setting the goals and direction for the
business and then restating them over and over and over again at
every level in the organization. She emphasized that she needed
to keep the goals simple so that they could be expressed in ways
that were just as meaningful to the most recently recruited
school-leaver on his or her first day in the company as they were
to her fellow directors.

She suggested that while this process could be supported by
online newsletters, mission and value statements, messages from
the chairman, cascade briefings and the myriad other organizational communication tools that can now be mustered, she
insisted that, at the end of the day, people needed to hear the
message personally, from her. It was, she said, her job to hold
together a loose agglomeration of creative and enthusiastic tal-
ent, ensuring that it was focused upon the company's core goals
and that these were never forgotten, not even for a moment. To
do this, these talented people had to see her and hear her say the
words, show the emotion and convince them of the convictions

upon which her plans were based. "It isn't enough to be right", she told us, "You have to be able to demonstrate the depth of your belief in the fact that you are right. It is a matter of heart rather than of head."

There would always be emergencies, opportunities, potential diversions and distractions. Some of these would arise from outside the business; others would be the result of internal enthusiasms, competition, organizational power struggles and personality differences. But her job, she said, was to ensure that overall the organization maintained direction and confidence in a "steady as she goes" approach.

This was never more important than at times of crisis. There were times, she told us, that she felt a strong wish to throw in the towel and to do something other than continually do the rounds of the business "singing the same song" over and over again.

It is tempting to think that you can delegate the role of "message giver" to someone else so that you can focus your attention on things that seem to be of higher priority, more challenging and more exciting. But maintaining clarity and consistency of purpose is one of the biggest challenges that organizational leaders face, because it is through your demonstrated consistency and clarity of purpose that you develop the commitment upon which the success of the organization will ultimately depend.

6.10   Integrated thinking: leadership and trust

While rational-analytic thinking and language are essential to an objective appreciation of the relationships between an organization's purpose, resources, technology and contextual position, over-dependence upon them can cause its leadership to appear cold and impersonal, exclusive and reductionist, legalistic and bureaucratic.

Imaginative-emotional thinking and language that makes use of anecdotes and stories, metaphor and humor and which generates empathy with people's feelings of happiness and fun, excitement and anxiety, sadness and discomfort are equally essential.

As leader of an organization you need to be multidimensional employing a form of thinking and language that integrates the rational-analytic with the imaginative-emotional. It is this that helps to establish that sense of presence that distinguishes the genuine leader from the individual who merely occupies a leadership role. The chasm between the two can be huge.

So, assuming that you have ensured that you have the "right people on the bus" (and, by implication, the wrong ones off) you must earn their commitment by trusting them to get on with whatever aspect of the overall task it is that you have assigned to them.

Trust begets trust, involving a willingness on the part of both parties to go at risk. As a leader you need to demonstrate that you say what you mean and that you mean what you say. You must be consistent in your behavior and, as we have seen, this involves you in being clear to yourself and to others about your values and the boundaries that you are unwilling to cross.

You will never be the fount of all wisdom and knowledge in your organization and sometimes you will make mistakes. By acknowledging your own, you will make it easier for those who work for you to admit to theirs. As we have already pointed out, we all have an unconscious tendency to model our behaviors on the behaviors of those who lead us.

Those who successfully occupy leadership roles over the long term gain reciprocal benefit by constructively questioning and challenging those whom they lead and by encouraging them to respond in kind, without diminishing or undermining their leadership authority.

Such reciprocal questioning facilitates experimentation and risk-taking within boundaries that are clearly stated and mutually held through being consistent, simple, well understood and constantly reinforced. Communication in a language that enables quite diverse groups of people to join together as whole human beings in pursuit of a set of common goals with which they can identify personally, offers far more far more than a toolkit with which to work or a snakepit in which to compete with one another.

Developing the internal organizational context in this way should be the goal of every organization's leader. But the internal context will soon become a handicap to effective performance if the organization's leadership fails to keep in touch with the signals that herald changes in its external context, to which we turn in chapter 7.

CHAPTER 7

Context is key

7.1 Keeping in touch with the external context

Throughout this book we have stressed how important it is for leaders of businesses or organizations to be aware of what is going on in the wider environment within which their business or organization is situated. The leader must be constantly on the lookout for signals and cues for possible changes or developing trends that may give rise to events that could be significant for the organization and its performance. We have discussed the importance of generating *"memories of the future"* through the use of techniques such as scenario planning so that the organization as a whole may become sensitive to such wider environmental trends and their possible implications. The use of such techniques and getting their messages into the organization's bloodstream by means of the myths and stories that are told within it greatly increase the chances that signals, even weak ones, that cue the arrival of the unexpected will be picked up and that the organization will respond appropriately.

In Chapter 3 we noted how the directors with whom Graham worked on his research into their roles as drivers of organizational change tended to define the change processes in which they were involved as "projects". For most of these directors such projects were discrete, time-bound entities that they saw as being something quite distinct and separate from their other ongoing responsibilities. Graham noted two dimensions in the ways that the directors managed these change projects. The first of these involved the director's *"personal focus."* Was his focus of attention turned *inwards* – giving emphasis to the project as something that was his personal responsibility; something that it was down to him to deliver and control and upon which his personal reputation and future was likely to depend? Or was his attention primarily focused *outwards* – emphasizing his role as one of integrating several different skill networks, coordinating their contributions within and to the benefit of the organization as a whole? In this perception, the director saw his role, though critical, as being contributory rather than primary. A keyword on the lips of the inwardly focused director was likely to be "I", while for the outwardly focused director it was much more likely to be "we".

The second dimension to the ways in which these directors led their change projects concerned what Graham called their "*contextual perspective.*" Was this perspective *internal* – largely confined within the boundaries of their own organization? Or was it essentially *external*, taking in the wider social, political, economic and technological environment in which the organization was located?

Of course, the locations of the directors on these two different dimensions were by no means mutually exclusive, and some of the directors changed their positions somewhat in response to circumstances. Nonetheless, each tended to express views and to demonstrate attitudes and behaviors that suggested one of the following four different positions:

- Personal focus: Inward   Contextual Perspective: Internal
- Personal focus: Outward   Contextual Perspective: Internal
- Personal focus: Inward   Contextual Perspective: External
- Personal focus: Outward   Contextual Perspective: External

Graham was struck by the fact that directors who tended to occupy the fourth location more than any of the others were likely to deal with the impact of unexpected events much more successfully, both at the organizational and the personal level. They were less likely to be caught off-guard; to respond more appropriately and to grasp the opportunities offered or to recover from setbacks than were the other three groups. Those whose personal focus was primarily inward directed and whose contextual perspective was essentially internal were much more likely to experience the impact of unexpected events negatively – as the following comments made by two directors in this group suggest:

> I was in shock. I couldn't come to terms with what had happened. In many ways I don't think that I have even now. Perhaps I never will … I desperately wanted to turn the clock back, to replace what I had lost.

> There are different ways of doing things, I suppose – an American way and a British way, I'm making no judgement. I am a naturally enthusiastic and infectious person. Probably it would have paid to be more low-key, less certain than I have been. I shoot from the hip and, therefore, I expose my back … err … I have been too outspoken, too trusting, too certain. If I hadn't been, I would probably be the Chairman of a large plc today. Yes, I was too outspoken and too sure that I knew what needed to be done.

In both these cases the directors concerned had failed to ensure that they kept in touch with the wider context in which they and their organizations were operating and in which changes occurred for which they were both were unprepared. Their inability to respond quickly and appropriately to such changes was to cost both of them their jobs.

Those directors who tended to adopt an outward personal focus together with an external contextual perspective were much more sensitive to trends in the environment, being much more aware of the bigger picture, taking a strategic, long-term view in their approach to the changes that they wished to bring about. They were constantly on the lookout for partnerships, alliances and opportunities for collaboration. Their approach was characterized by flexibility, accommodation and constant adaptation. While their counterparts (whose personal focus was directed inwards and whose contextual perspective was largely confined within the boundaries of their own organization) tended to be much more concerned with bringing their short-term projects to a successful conclusion as quickly as possible, getting involved in details that they believed would ensure short-term "wins", chalking up their successes and striving to be winners in the inevitable games of organizational politics.

If you are to make sense of what is going on in the world, you need to be always on the lookout for the signals and clues that that world offers you. You are much more likely to understand the significance of unexpected events if you can see them in their wider context. If you fail to do so, you will miss those signals and cues that might give you advance warning of unexpected events. It is then that such events are likely to take you by surprise and cause you to make decisions and to take actions that you come to regret.

7.2   The external context: 2015?

As we write this chapter, the global economy is teetering on the brink of depression or worse. A predictable turn of the economic cycle away from explosive growth to slow-down, fueled by the availability of cheap and easy credit together with the economic energies, low labor costs, and booming consumerism of China and India, has been greatly exacerbated by what is now revealed to have been a willingness on the part first of US and then European banks to extend credit to a level that verged upon the insane. The consequence of this apparent insanity has been the generation of unsustainable levels of "toxic" (i.e. bad) debt on an unprecedented scale. Banks that were previously revered as paragons of financial rectitude and probity have collapsed and many of those that have not done so owe their survival to the injections of billions of dollars, euros and pounds' worth of public money that has meant the effective nationalization of some of free market capitalism's greatest financial institutions.

So a predictable slow-down of the global economic cycle has been transformed into meltdown. Each day brings further media reports of businesses that have long provided the engines of economic growth and development going bust or pleading for government bailouts to prevent or perhaps delay their doing so. Manufacturing and retailing jobs are disappearing by the million as are those in the banking and financial services sector within which the amplification of the troubles appeared to begin.

It is against this background that we are stressing the importance of staying in touch with the wider context within which your business is operating and against the background of which you must endeavor to lead your organization. You could be forgiven for thinking that this is about as sensible as suggesting that you might be well advised to dress warmly when going out into a snowstorm – yet another statement of the patently obvious. But all too often we see organizational leaders responding to the crisis by battening down the hatches, withdrawing to the apparent safety of their core businesses, forgetting that the customers of these businesses are facing the same threats and challenges and, by their actions, further changing the context within which their business operates.

Economists and politicians first advised us that we are entering the deepest recession, since the early nineteen nineties. It then became the worst since the early nineteen eighties; since the late or early nineteen seventies; then since the nineteen sixties. As of today they have not actually mentioned the year 1929 and the Wall Street Crash in their gloomy predictions although that event is increasingly mentioned in media programmes and articles analysing our present situation. They continue to argue amongst themselves as to just how deep the recession will be and how long it will be before the shape of the post recession economy starts to reveal itself.

But we would like to suggest that battening down the hatches and waiting for recovery is the kind of strategy that spells doom for the inwardly focused director with an internal contextual perspective. It represents a "stuff happens" attitude, a lack of strategic intent and responsibility, reflecting the hope that, one day, things will go back to normal.

They won't.

We are not futurologists but we do believe that there are some very clear signs – for which the evidence has been around for years, if not for decades – that suggest that the world beyond the recession that began in 2008, and that the new normality that will follow it will show an acceleration of some of the trends that preceded it.

Here are a few suggestions as to what the world post recession, perhaps sometime beyond 2015, might look like:

7.1 A post-credit-crunch world

- Past recessions have seen the ongoing decline of traditional manufacturing in the UK, there is little to suggest that this decline will not continue in the present one. At the start of the 2008 downturn, manufacturing accounted for approximately 13 percent of the UK's gross domestic product. This could be down to single figures at the recession's end.
- Globalization has been the name of the economic game for well over a decade. Its driving force and Master of Ceremonies has been the USA. Post recession, the economic influence on the world economy of the USA, while still huge, will certainly be somewhat less than it is at present. In contrast, the influence of China, India, the revitalized so-called tiger economies (South Korea, Malaysia, Taiwan and Singapore) and Japan will be significantly greater and their drivers will be keen to exercise their economic muscles. While the voices of protectionism will grow louder during the recession, the tide of globalization is unlikely to be reversed. However the location of its major beneficiaries is likely to continue to move towards the East.
- The experience of global recession, energy shortages and the vulnerability of its supply, together with a greater recognition of the threat to human societies posed by global warming, particularly in poorer, southern countries is likely to encourage the growth of both political extremism and religious fundamentalism. This in turn will have its impact upon democratic societies, increasing the threat of terrorist attack and presenting a considerable challenge to the preservation of rights that have been taken for granted for years. This will raise the political temperature in all societies.

- The pressures of what psychologist, Oliver James has termed "*Affluenza*" and "*Selfish Capitalism*"[1] that have been driving those who dwell in Anglo-Saxon communities to work incredibly long hours in order to be able to "have" rather than in order to "be", may well go into a decline. Even before the credit crunch and the discrediting of the banks that generated it, many people were beginning to seriously question what working to excess meant for their quality of life, despite the gargantuan salaries and bonuses that this way of life appeared to offer. Such people were either downshifting or giving such an option their serious consideration. The experience of redundancy and unemployment will provide a great many more people with the opportunity to downshift without having the luxury of having given it much prior consideration. Many of these people are likely to find the different pace of life, though less endowed with the material advantages of affluence, much more personally satisfying and rewarding in terms of quality of life. This is even more likely to be the case amongst those who feel let down, disenchanted, if not exactly screwed, by their former city and multinational employers.
- Many of those who retain their jobs are likely to experience the guilt and feelings of anxiety that has been described as "survivor syndrome" – "How come I have managed to keep my job while friends and colleagues whom I regard as being at least as capable as I am, if not more so, have lost theirs?" The morale levels, motivation and, therefore, the commitment of such survivors are likely to be low.
- Many household business names (especially in manufacturing and retail) will not be around to see the economy recover.
- There is likely to be a greatly increased gulf between the big name supermarkets and retail chains and small boutique-style businesses, many of which will quickly come and go and others of which will prove to be the entrepreneurial drivers of the economy in the second quarter of the twenty-first century. Most of these businesses do not exist at present and many of their owners

are still in school or as yet unborn. A majority of these businesses is likely to be internet-based and located away from traditional commercial centers of employment. Many will have a relatively brief "half life" and perform like shooting stars, briefly burning brightly before disappearing altogether.

- The most successful, sustainable of these new businesses will be knowledge and information driven, highly responsive to the demands of an unstable society and capable of demonstrating high levels of flexibility and with the capacity to rapidly reconfigure themselves when the situation demands. Their employees are likely to come and go both in response to the uncertain economic situation upon which many such organizations will thrive and because such businesses will not offer them, nor will they expect them to provide, long-term employment let alone a career.

- A majority of the post recession generation of workers will be more highly educated than those trying to enter employment at its beginning, but will not expect their education to provide them with any guarantee of employment. They will need to anticipate changing their chosen career path at least twice in their working life, during which time they will experience several periods of unemployment. To reduce the length of such periods they will need to return to education and training several times over the course of their working lives.

- The major drivers of the economy will be, as at present, small and medium sizes businesses employing fewer than fifty people.

- Those in employment or who have successfully squirreled away their pre-recession, bonus-based wealth will find that they are expected to pay considerably higher levels of tax than they have been accustomed to paying:
  - First, to repay the huge government borrowings that were required to enable the economy to survive the recession.
  - Second, to finance high levels of ongoing unemployment (albeit much of it proving to be short-term)

and the education and training required to reduce unemployment towards levels that are politically and economically sustainable.

- third, to provide for the health care of the increasing percentage of the population that will be no longer in employment (despite a later retirement age), in increasingly poor health and requiring more and more expensive care as its life expectancy increases while medical science finds ever more inventive ways of prolonging it even further.
- Finally, to fund the major changes to infrastructure that will be required as we are driven with increasing velocity towards a post-carbon economy.

Many if not most of the leaders of post-recession business organizations will have attained their positions through the kinds of routes pursued by the Richard Bransons, Steve Jobs and Bill Gates of the world, though only a very few will do so quite so spectacularly. They will have started small, founding their own businesses, nurturing them and growing them into successful empires at the head of which they may well not choose to remain. They will have made their own rules of organization design and behavior, forged their own principles of leadership and will not have served their time in career organizations or as salary men and women in large, traditional corporations.

Other successful small- and medium-sized businesses will have been created by serial entrepreneurs – like those who now sit in a row of chairs within a somewhat forbidding loft, watching and listening in television's Dragon's Den, while aspiring inventors and would-be creators of start-up businesses plead with them for pump priming finance and support in exchange for a piece of their equity and, probably, of their souls. The leaders of such businesses will need to pay particular attention to the expectations and demands of their entrepreneurial stakeholders if they are not to experience a succession of unexpected and unwelcome events at their behest as their serial entrepreneurial benefactors find and move on to pastures new.

No, things will not go back to normal.

7.3 The external context – competitors and suppliers

It used to be the case that a major company could be pretty clear about where it stood in relation to its competitors. Businesses tended to form communities that were quite limited in their membership. Like professional communities of practice, the members of such industry or trading groups tended to know one another personally and appreciate one another's foibles, their individual strengths and weaknesses. As a result, together with the help of a little well-directed market intelligence, it was a relatively straightforward task (although sometimes an expensive one) to find out what one's competitors were up to and to formulate or amend one's own strategies and tactics accordingly.

However a combination of the globalization of markets and the great acceleration of the rate of technological development has revealed the limitations to such "clubby" competitive thinking. As we have already stated, many of tomorrow's major competitors to your business do not exist today, while recession will ensure that many of today's competitors will not be around tomorrow.

Be sure to honor your suppliers by understanding their goals, their anxieties and the threats to their own survival. The battles for supermarket dominance that have been a major feature of the UK business in recent years have damaged many of their suppliers in the crossfire of competitive cost-cutting between the warring parties. Some supermarkets have been unwise enough to turn on their suppliers, forcing them to accept terms of trade that put their survival at risk even before recession and the drying up of credit lines put them at additional risk.

The cavalier response of the supermarkets to their suppliers' protests, that they (the supermarkets) could always go to someone else, may have confirmed to the suppliers that, in the short-term at least they have had no alternative other than to accept their terms. Recession may cause some supermarkets to turn on their suppliers once again. This may be of help to the supermarkets in the short-term, but it will also actively encourage many more of those suppliers who survive to seek ways to ensure that they are never caught the same way twice. Inevitably, some will be driven out of business or conclude that the business is no longer one in which they wish to remain. As one former supermarket supplier, now specializing in supplying his internet customers with a limited range of high-quality organic produce, commented ruefully, "*The supermarkets might note that some pips will piss off before they are squeezed to death and that, in any case, dead pips can't squeak.*"

The steady growth in and popularity of farmer's markets is not simply part of a trend towards the consumption of locally produced organic food on the part of drivers of Chelsea tractors in green wellies and Barbour jackets, but evidence perhaps of worms turning as the supermarkets' suppliers have sought ways to lessen their dependency upon them. Recession might well cause this trend to slow down but we are sure that thereafter it will accelerate apace along with the desire to downshift that recession will also encourage.

7.4   Sensitivity to external signals

As leader of a competitive business you must constantly be sensitive to the signals provided not only by your competitors and suppliers but to those that come from the wider external environment generally. Sometimes such signals may be very weak; barely impinging upon your consciousness but pick them up you must, storing them away as memories for the future that you and your colleagues may draw upon when circumstances provide you with an unexpected opportunity or threat. If you do not, you may be certain that someone else will do so, and that this will not be to your benefit.

Staying in touch with context is a key responsibility of any organizational leader, and cannot be maintained if you are constantly driven by a need to be personally involved in organizational detail, a need to be seen as in charge, and a need to exercise personal control. These things may largely be delegated while the integrative role of leadership can never be. We are often saddened by the behaviors of many of those who have risen to positions of organizational leadership from ones of supervision and management. They continue to engage with organizational minutiae, seeking to demonstrate that they are in charge of everything.

This might just have been appropriate behavior lower down the ladder but it is foolish for any organizational leader because it is to attempt the impossible. The only thing worse than a director behaving as though he or she were still a manager is the director who has never been a manager believing that now he can become one! The roles of leader and of director are very different from those of manager.

This returns us to the paradox that if you wish to remain in control you must be willing to let it go, having ensured that you have worked to develop a climate of mutual trust, common values, a shared vision and are confident that you have the "right people on the bus" who will do the managing for you.

Picking up signals, no matter how weak, from your business's wider environment is less likely if your time is dominated by managing or by a personal focus that is inwardly directed, driving you to take action that leaves you no time for listening, sensing and reflecting.

The signals to which the organizational leader's antennae need to be sensitive are widely differing and may very well be conflicting. The leader needs space and time for reflection in order to note, interpret, make sense of and store those signals and their possible implications. Those signals that are most at risk of being drowned out by stronger ones are particularly important. As leader of your organization you need to be able to rise above the clamor, while never becoming totally detached from it. You need also to beware of the siren songs of those who will tell you only that which they think you may prefer to hear.

Unfortunately, it is inevitable that such people will be at the forefront of those who will be making claims upon your attention, promoting either the maintenance of the status quo, or encouraging the pursuit of initiatives in new directions, of which weaker signals from the outside could be warning you to beware.

Newcomers to tomorrow's markets won't come up with cheaper, more efficient mouse traps, they will change the ways in which people think about mice, perhaps persuading them to buy food for them instead of traps. This is a rather clumsy way of saying that the kinds of changes that are in the offing will require you to be constantly rethinking your underlying business models and to be prepared to adjust and reconfigure your organization, not just while you are doing your best to get through the crisis of recession but on a regular and recurrent basis.

Thus, the brewery group that we mentioned in the previous chapter took the decision to move further down the supply chain, recasting itself as a broadly based player in the leisure and hospitality business, eventually getting out of brewing altogether. On some occasions such rethinking may require you to take steps that are so radical as to appear unthinkable to your colleagues. This was certainly true in the case of the top management of the brewing group. Selling off the breweries was such a significant step, that it would have been impossible had not the chief executive had the vision, the conviction, the passion and the enthusiasm to persuade his board colleagues and senior managers to join him in contemplating the unthinkable. He could only develop and apply these emotional strengths having patiently and diligently gathered the necessary evidence as a result of picking up the signals from the external environment.

Many years ago, the leaders of Kimberley Clark in the US and Metal Box in the UK similarly decided to sell off their core businesses (paper mills and metal cans respectively) because they could see no long-term path to strength and growth by staying with them. In both cases, went their leaders' reasoning, the future held out the prospect of the companies' having to fight rearguard, survival actions against traditional, competing manufacturers within shrinking markets, coupled with a need to deal with aggressive interventions by newcomers from new and developing markets and by yet others with entirely new and alternative products and processes. These business leaders, Darwin Smith at Kimberley Clark and Brian Smith at Metal Box, were both heavily criticized for their decisions to get out of their companies' core businesses as being akin to *"selling the family silver"*. But, by taking these bold decisions, both men freed their companies to move away from defensive, on-the-back-foot strategies in favor of ones that proved to be both liberating and creative. These strategies, successfully and enthusiastically pursued, enabled both companies to be reinvigorated and to go on to new and different kinds of success in areas of business that were only loosely connected to their original core.

The emphasis in this chapter thus far has been upon paying attention to the external context in which your business operates. We have argued that a tendency towards being inwardly focused and an over-concern with the internal contextual perspective is highly dangerous, since it can cause you to be caught out by external events whose possible impact you had not anticipated.

You can also, of course, go too far the other way, paying too little attention to the *internal* context within which your business operates, a context that is largely determined by the processes, policies and procedures that it has built up over time.

7.5 Keeping in touch with the internal context: process

As the leader of your organization you must appreciate the importance of *process* – the ways in which things are done within your organization, just as well as the things that the organization delivers; its outputs. Here we are talking about the, "*hows*" rather than the, "*whats*" of your business.

At one level, a concern for process is very much a matter of style ("the way that we do things round here"), while at another it is a great deal more formal, including all the systems and procedures that convert the inputs A, B, C ...^{n} into the outputs X, Y, Z ...^{q}.

We don't suggest for a moment that newly appointed leaders should avoid taking any action prior to their having developed an in-depth appreciation of each and every one of the many detailed processes and procedures upon which the operation of the business is likely to have come to depend. Clearly, even if that were possible, it would be inappropriately time consuming!

However, we do argue, and we argue very strongly, that the leader who goes into action in the absence of a well developed *sense* of the style and processes by means of which things are made to happen in the organization is very unwise.

7.6   Representations of the internal context

We keep returning to the gap that seems to exist between the formal manner and language in which we represent the management challenges and problems that we face and the more esoteric, personal and imaginative ways that we experience such challenges in practice. For example, we typically represent our organization in terms a triangle in two dimensions thus:

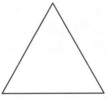

Figure 7.1   The organizational pyramid

Providing us with the basis for the typical organogram or organization chart employed in many organizations to represent its different functions, roles and responsibilities, thus:

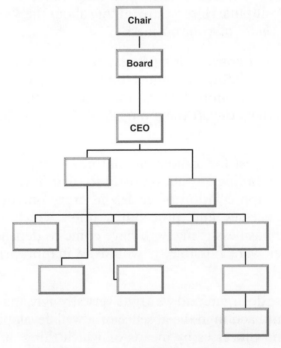

Figure 7.2   A classic organogram

With the recent explosive developments in organizational information processing capacity and capability, such pyramids have
become increasingly shallow, representing the trend to fewer, flatter
structures that are characterized by group and team working rather
than by the traditional command and control models, thus:

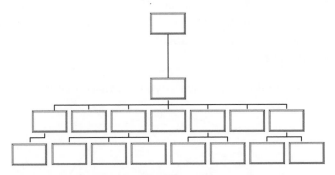

Figure 7.3 Flatter structures, reduced hierarchies

The impact of this trend in organization design has been discussed
in many books of management and organizational theory, some
of which emphasize the need for excellent lateral or cross-the-
organizational communication processes as a means for achieving organizational effectiveness through well integrated specialist
functions. As we have seen, the different "languages" employed
within such specialisms can make communication difficult and
ineffective in the absence of a leader who is skilled in providing an
integrated form of communication that effectively links the rational-analytical and imaginative-emotional modes of thinking.

We might decide to change the representation of the organizational pyramid, first from one dimension to two, like this:

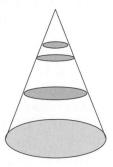

Figure 7.4 The organization in two dimensions

The perception that we now have of the organizational pyramid becomes a little more complex and open to interpretation. For example, we could ask ourselves whether the above pyramid is standing vertically or if it is leaning towards or away from us. The opportunity for different people to interpret the organizational representation has been increased. But this is not to say that such differences in interpretation do not exist in actual organizations, only that traditional representations have tended to hide or suppress such differences.

Or perhaps we could take a bird's eye view of our organization thus:

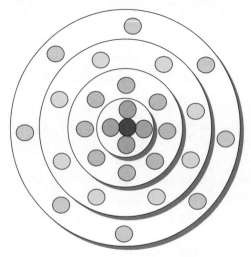

Figure 7.5   A bird's eye organogram?

We now acquire an organizational insight that is quite different from that provided by the two-dimensional "flatland" perspective offered by the conventional organizational chart that is perfectly straightforward, logical and rational.

When we look at the bird's eye representation of an organization that is offered by the previous figure, each of the concentric circles might be said to represent a managerial tier or level of the organization, while each of the dots within each circle might represent a function or role, with the CEO being represented by the dot at the very center of all the circles. We might also recognize that none of the circles or dots is ever entirely static but, like molecules in a suspension, is in a constant state of Brownian motion as relationships, power positions, etc. constantly shift and adjust giving rise to the kinds of "snakepit" experiences described in the previous chapter.

Linking this view of the organization to our discussion of organizational language and communication in Chapter 6, we would suggest that each of the functional dots has its own particular jargon, professional standards and values and, therefore, its own "language" that differs in subtle ways from those of all the other functions. The technical term for what we are here calling "languages" is a discourse, the total mix of spoken, written and behavioral exchanges that is characteristic of a particular group of people and which, therefore, distinguishes that group from all others.

Within these functional discourses or languages there will be further subtle variations that reflect membership of the different organizational levels at which the function is represented. Nevertheless these languages still have much in common with one another. It is quite apparent, therefore, that the communication networks that exist within complex organizations are themselves highly complex.

A key role of the chief executive is to ensure that these complex networks are sufficiently well integrated to enable the organization to operate effectively.

But, of course, life is even more complex than this. No organization exists in isolation and so the representation of the internal network shows only part of the story. It forms part of a myriad other inter-organizational communication and other networks, each of which is as complex and as full of subtle variations as are those within the original organization.

The figure below indicates some of the typical, interdependent internal and external networks with which organizational leaders are likely to find themselves regularly engaged. Within such networks you will need to be able to communicate effectively in ways that make sense to participants from different backgrounds and with different priorities. You will need to be sensitive to the subtle differences in the "languages" that are employed by participants in each of the different networks:

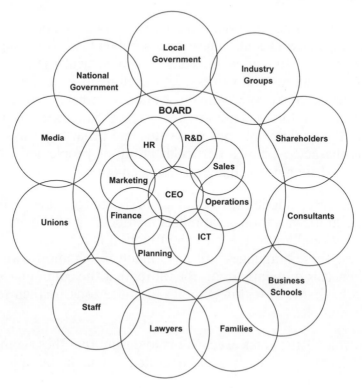

Figure 7.6   Some typical networks of a CEO

As an organizational leader you occupy a critical nodal point where, argues Madeleine Bunting[2] (2004), information needs to be *"accurately analysed, decisions made and power lies, but this is also where information overload is at its most acute."*

How do people occupying such "nodal points" deal with the overload and the infinite and subtle complexity of the information and communication requirements with which they are confronted?

When Graham researched the experiences of the nine directors on which this book is partly based, he found that the requirement to manage information overload was one of the pressures that caused the directors to endeavor to break down the complexity into discrete and apparently more manageable "chunks", segments or projects, each of which could then be considered as being more or less self-contained. By focusing upon a limited number of such segments or projects at any one time, while keeping the complexity and overload of the whole mesh of interconnected networks in the background but, nevertheless, in mind, some of these directors were able to make sense of the range and volume of information in which they were constantly immersed while maintaining a focus on their overall goals and plans and staying in touch with both the internal and external contexts within which they were operating.

But in the process of so doing, as we have noted, it emerged that some of them ran considerable risks. Narrowing their focus from the network as a whole to what, at a particular point in time, they considered to be the most critical few of its more significant parts, could leave them dangerously unprepared to deal with unexpected events that only made sense within the context of the network as a whole.

The incredible outpourings of creative imagination that have been unleashed by the power of computer graphics and gaming technology have demonstrated that there are tremendous opportunities for representing how we might visualize and reconfigure our organizations in radically new and exciting ways. Taking advantage of these opportunities not only provides you with the scope to develop entirely new kinds of organization but also for reshaping and redesigning existing ones in ways that may unleash resources for innovation that were previously untapped, unexploited and unimagined. But taking advantage of such opportunities will require you to let go of previous conceptions about what organizations "ought" to look like.

7.7   Stuff goes right on happening

Given the complexity of the networks within which you have to operate it is abundantly clear that you cannot possibly exercise control over anything much more than a very small part of the total. But it is also clear that your leadership decisions and actions will often be in response to unexpected events that have occurred elsewhere in the network and over which there is very little chance that you could exercise any influence at all, let alone have controlled.

The decisions that you must to take in order to enable you to manage and make greater sense of the limited number of segments or projects over which you have chosen to exercise your influence and control may, unless you take great care, render you *less* sensitive to the significance of the unexpected events that are occurring elsewhere in the network. Such events happen all the time.

As a business or organizational leader, you will need to ensure that you are visible; you need to be the embodiment of the organization, its goals and its values to its internal and external stakeholders. You will also need to do a great deal of looking and listening, as opposed to talking, prior to going into action. This is essential if you are to know, really know, your business, its people, the processes upon which it depends while at the same time remaining in touch with different stakeholders within the organization (the internal context) and within the wider, external context in which it operates.

It is unlikely that you will be able to achieve all of this without being willing and able to bring about a number of major changes within your organization. Our experience and the evidence of a considerable volume of academic research suggest that a majority of organizational change efforts fail to bring about the benefits that the change-makers expected of it. Why might this be?

7.8   Making changes that work

A majority of changes within organizations are experienced as having been imposed upon those who are going to have to make them work. Not surprisingly people who feel that they have been imposed upon tend to feel aggrieved and resistant to those who are calling for change.

A great deal has been written about "overcoming resistance to change". But, it seems to us, this misses the point. It would be far better to avoid incurring the resistance in the first place, as far as you possibly can.

By and large people do not resist change but they do take exception to having it done to them. They also do not take kindly to having their intelligence insulted by organizational announcements from their chief executive that suggest that by making sacrifices now (i.e. you) the organization (i.e. me) will emerge stronger and healthier, better able to meet the challenges of the future. This is simply another excuse for avoiding the difficult conversation. It is why people are "let go" rather than being made redundant or fired.

Change works well when it is conducted with honesty and confidence when it meets a number of criteria such as those that follow.

- Organizational changes work when they come about as clear responses to environmental conditions and contextual events that provide opportunities for growth or threats to organizational survival. They rarely work well when they are driven simply by a desire to improve or when they are imposed. You cannot pull yourself up by your own bootstraps.
- Unless those people who are going to be affected by the change can be provided with a view of what life in the changed organization is going to be like and what will be in it for them, they are unlikely to be enthused by it. For some people, the change will be unacceptable or there may not be a place for them in the changed structure. Such people need to be treated with honesty, compassion and support.
- When John relocated his company's headquarters from Berkshire to the Midlands, those who would not be making the move or who chose not to make it were kept as fully in the picture about the changes as those who were going to move to the new HQ; they were encouraged and assisted to acquire new skills that would make them more marketable when they came to leave; some of them had their job titles modified (or enriched) for the same reasons or were offered financial, loyalty incentives. Very few left before the move and nearly all joined in the celebratory parties that were held when the change project was at an end.

- If you as the organization's leader are dissatisfied with its current situation, you need to act in order to ensure that your sense of dissatisfaction is as widely shared as possible. You also need to share a specific vision of the ways in which you believe things will be better after the changes have been made. Simply stating that your slimmed down organization will be fitter and better able to meet the challenges of the future is to speak in weasel words. People in your organization need to feel dissatisfied with the status quo and have a genuine belief that things will be better, even if they themselves may not get to play a part in them.

- A great many organizational changes come to grief because it is believed that they can be made to work like clockwork and be implemented in one, single big bang. Big bangs are frequently associated with things being blown up and this is often the case with organizational changes of the big bang variety. Organizations are systems and introducing a change in one part of a system will produce "knock-on" changes in every other part of the system. Therefore it is well to recognize that change tends to progress through different parts of an organization at different rates, and is more successful when it is acknowledged that it is going to be messy and is managed accordingly.

- Any change is always uncomfortable and frequently painful even for those who are deeply committed to the change and who have been driving to make it happen. Recognize this from the outset rather than deny it and treat those who are suffering as a consequence of the changes for which you are striving with compassion and understanding. But remember to identify saboteurs and remove them swiftly but with dignity.

- The more complex the change, the more likely you are to benefit from the support of both internal and external experts. Within the organization such people are likely to be those who are closest to the site of the change, though they will not necessarily occupy particularly senior positions. Therefore they may not naturally come to the fore with their contributions (unless you have already established a climate where this is encouraged). Do not fall into the trap of berating the lowly employee who knew that your propositions would not work but did not tell you, when you have never taken the trouble to ask.

- External consultants should be engaged on the basis of the contribution they can make and never as a comfort blanket provided by their image and reputation. Never, ever give them the accountability for making the change happen. That is your responsibility and one that cannot be delegated. Consultants live to fight another day, organizational leaders may not.
- Remember that no two organizations are the same and, therefore, that every change is unique. You can learn from what other organizations are doing or from what they have done, but you cannot simply take what they have done and apply it to your own organization with its unique tone, circumstances and situation. This is why changes that are driven by someone brought in with a glowing reputation for changes that he or she has implemented with success elsewhere, frequently fail to meet their expectations. Change isn't something that can be simply lifted from the shelf.
- Change works well when it is visibly led by the person at the top of the organization and driven on down through the line management chain. Change agents and specialists in change management from an HR function may be helpful and supportive but you and the line must own the change or it will not succeed.
- People sometimes make the mistake of seeing change as something temporary and that once "this" change has been completed things will go back to normal. They won't. Change is normality. It is ongoing, endless and will go on forever.

So how will you know that your particular change has avoided all these pitfalls, is delivering what you required of it and that your organization really is in a healthier state than it was when you embarked upon the process of making the changes?

Apart from the more obvious and measurable changes, such as productivity having gone up and costs having gone down, there is another very useful and indirect indicator of successful change.

This is that change that works tends to result in channels of communication being more open, the tone of the organization becoming more supportive, positive and negative feedback being more readily given both up and down the organization. While the process of change is always painful, when it is well led, it can result in a significant improvement in organizational climate by generating higher levels of openness, candor and trust.

This too can be uncomfortable for those in positions of leadership.

7.9 Pulling the threads together

In writing this book, we have focused our attention on exploring some of the ways in which leaders deal with unexpected events and their consequences. Inevitably some leaders handle the unexpected better than others, while yet other, otherwise successful, leaders appear to be totally thrown when the unexpected happens. We asked ourselves why this might be and what were the kinds of things that might lead to these different responses.

We might have decided to launch ourselves into a serious piece of research (Graham has, after all, spent much of his working life doing just that). However, we really wanted to look back over our own, very different experiences. Then, having reflected upon and discussed those experiences at length, we wished to draw some conclusions of our own and to discover what we had learned.

Perhaps the single and most important thing that we have learned is that the ways in which people respond to the unexpected has very little to do with the unexpected event itself. Our reactions to the unexpected are largely determined by a number of factors most of which have something to do with the leaders themselves and that were in place way before the event occurred.

Now as we are drawing the book to its conclusion, we wish to summarize the various issues that we have explored in the preceding pages, singling out those factors that seem to us to play a significant role in shaping the ways in which you as a leader of your organization are likely to respond to the unexpected when it happens.

First of all, those leaders who deal successfully with unexpected events are *well prepared.* They are rarely taken by surprise. Why?

- They are highly self-aware and are very clear about their personal values – the things that they are prepared to do and those things that they are not; where they might be willing to compromise and where they never will. *They know who they are* and can identify the touchstones, the fixed points by which they navigate their way through an environment that is highly complex, unstable and highly uncertain.

- They never lose touch with what is happening within that environment, the wider context within which their business and organizations must operate. They recognize its instability and risks and never take them for granted.

- They have confidence and conviction with regard to their aims and objectives, but are comfortable to operate within an environment in which their confidence and their convictions are subject to continuous challenge. They are not significantly rattled by ambiguity, contradiction or paradox.

- They are happy to exercise choice in four interrelated areas of challenge when leading their organizations:

  - To build structures and develop processes and procedures that are both logically based, being derived from a sound analysis of the demands arising from the organization's goals and purpose and from the environment in which it operates, and which also make sense and are meaningful at a practical and emotional level.

  - To ensure that they are clear about and aware of the personal attitudes, prejudices and values that they hold, knowing that these will be reflected in their behavior and, thus, in the values-in-use within the organizations that they lead. There is a high level of correlation between what they *say* they do and what they do (and are seen to be doing) in practice.

  - Whatever their particular leadership style may be (we do not believe that there is any one best style of leadership – only that there are styles that are more or less appropriate to their situation and circumstances), they are consistent in the way in which they apply it, regardless of who they happen to be dealing with. Through the example that they set by their behavior, they largely determine the tone of the organizations that they lead. In this they have no choice.

– To maintain their levels of self-awareness and self-insight, leaders who deal with unexpected events in the most effective ways make time for reflection and constructive, critical self-examination, often with the help and support of a trusted mentor – someone independent who is willing to tell them how it is, someone to hold up the mirror with honesty and without flinching. Such leaders have often enhanced their self-awareness by exploring their psychological type and preferences through the use of proprietary psychometric instruments.

The fact that you will be hit by unexpected events is inevitable. Regardless of whether such events represent opportunities or threats, they will always present a challenge to you and your plans. But they may be anticipated even if you do not know precisely what form they will take or when and how they will occur. If you can anticipate them, then you can prepare yourself to meet them.

- By learning to distinguish between unexpected events that are "*genuine*" and those that are a cumulative consequence of earlier errors, neglect or failure and to be on the lookout for or to notice signals of the unexpected and to encourage others to look out for them as well.
- By making the unexpected welcome, as something which provides opportunities for learning and to strengthen both your leadership and your organization, while fully recognizing that it is likely to be uncomfortable.
- By avoiding the temptation to look for someone to blame for the unfortunate consequences of unexpected events, seeking instead to understand what has happened, to learn from it and to benefit from such learning.
- By focusing attention on developing the solution rather than on the problem.
- By recognizing that much of the expertise necessary to finding an effective solution is likely to reside close to the area of impact of the unexpected event, but that such expertise may not be recognized or acknowledged. By not automatically reaching for or hiding behind consultants.
- By being constantly on the lookout for signs of *hubris* and by recognizing good luck for the good luck that it is, rather than

seeing it as evidence of your wisdom, intelligence and skill – and by never committing the sin of believing in your own bullshit.

- By listening to and by learning from the stories and myths that circulate within your organization, especially those that feature you. What do they tell you?
- By checking your assumptions and, when managing by exception, avoiding the trap of believing that the absence of ringing alarm bells or complaints signifies that all is well.
- By reviewing your policies, processes and procedures regularly and ensuring that they are relevant to your business and fit for purpose.
- By being professional and by playing by the rules while ensuring that you remain human, with human feelings and human failings.
- By integrating your rational-analytical thinking processes with your emotional-imaginative ones in order to stimulate your creativity, innovation and your powers of communication. By taking care not to be seduced by the language of either the toolkit or that of the snakepit.
- By ensuring that all the different resources upon which you depend are aligned and that they are pulling in the same direction.
- By remembering and honoring your obligations to:
  - Set and always be aware of the tone that you are setting for your organization.
  - Shape your organization's future by setting its direction and by generating "*memories of the future*" that will assist the organization to stay on course, anticipate the unexpected and stay on course towards its achievement.
  - Remain constantly in touch with both the internal and the external contexts, studying and developing your understanding of emergent trends, sources of uncertainty and their potential implications.
  - Do everything you can to develop and build upon the commitment of *all* your stakeholders.

Meanwhile, develop your ability and readiness to engage in difficult conversations, particularly when you need to hold such conversations with those who are, or who have been, close to you. Each such conversation delayed increases the likelihood of its becoming a conversation avoided. *NB This does not mean that you should not prepare for it.*

Finally, be careful not to fall into the trap of kidding yourself and attempting to persuade others that everything will be OK when things "go back to normal." They won't, because constant change is the current and future normality. So have the courage to embrace and to lead change successfully.

Now to action.

CHAPTER 8

Securing the ladder – preparing your action plan

8.1 By way of introduction

We hope that in the preceding seven chapters we have gained your attention and that we may have been thought-provoking. Your next step is to prepare for action. We cannot tell you what actions you should take – the buck really does stop with you and, of course, only you are in a position to make well-informed judgements about your own business, its future, its people and its stakeholders. However, we do hope that we may have given you some insight into the issues that surround the occurrence of unexpected events which will help you to focus your thinking.

The questions are – what actions do you need to take to:

- Find out where your unsecured ladders are?
- Minimize the occurrence and the effects of harmful unexpected events, especially those that are the unintended or cumulative consequence of earlier action or inaction?
- Maximize the benefits to be gained from opportunities that may arise as consequences of unexpected events?

In this brief final chapter we have grouped the issues together into eight areas so that you may start to formulate your answers to these questions.

These areas involve:

- Making time for reflection
- Holding up and looking into the mirror

- Checking the tone of the organization
- People
- Making changes that work
- Articulating the changing context
- Recognizing speed as a core competence
- Articulating your values and your personal touchstones

It is, of course, highly unlikely that working through the above on a one-off basis will deliver all or even most of the answers but it should provide you with a list of actions and initiatives that, when taken together, can begin to have a positive effect in assisting you to strengthen the organization, and your position in it, by helping you to ensure that your own personal ladder has been properly secured.

We anticipate that you would want to visit this list regularly, reviewing your answers to the questions each time and updating the actions that you decide to take, before resetting their priorities.

As always you will find yourself performing a number of balancing acts, such as keeping it simple while, at the same time, not being superficial; focusing on a few initiatives and making them a success rather than starting many things simultaneously and failing on most in consequence. We hope that you will take time to establish milestones and metrics of various kinds so that your progress can be assessed and measured and that this will become a matter of course to you.

You own and are accountable for all these actions and initiatives but remember to delegate wherever possible, and capture the natural enthusiasm of those whom you involve whenever you do.

8.2   Make time for reflection

8.2.1   The objective: to focus your impact on the organization

The unexpected is inevitable therefore if you are not to miss an opportunity or become a victim of events it is essential to prepare.

Stand back and take time out to take stock.

Adopt an attitude of constructive dissatisfaction.

Develop a scheme for benchmarking; purposeful networking can be a useful method for providing yourself with the information you need to do this.

Determine what needs to be changed or improved.

Check the quality of the information that you are receiving – is it accurate, complete and fit for purpose?

Are you measuring the right things?

How robust or vulnerable is your business and your business plan?

Are you building on the strengths?

Are you taking action to mitigate the weaknesses?

Use scenario planning.

Remember if you are surfing the wave of euphoria – get off the surfboard and take a long, hard, honest and objective look to learn how you got to this happy state. Did you make it happen or was it serendipity? What action should you take to maintain it?

8.3　Hold up and look into the mirror

8.3.1　The objective: improving your performance

Articulate your personal values.

What effect are they having on the organization, on its tone and its performance? What does this tell you?

What are your personal goals and aspirations? Do you have a self-development plan?

When did you last update it?

How well does it match with the goals and aspirations you have for the business?

Are you sacrificing your personal goals in order to meet those that you have set for the business? Are you sure that they are worth it?

Do you participate in training for your top team?

Do you use 360-degree feedback and appraisals?

Do you ask for feedback from your peers?

Would such feedback reports say you are consistent and that your reactions are for the most part predictable?

Do you have a mentor?

Do you tend to ask questions rather than give opinions?

Do you listen closely to the answers – are you an active listener?

How much of your time do you devote to seeing what's going on in your organization?

You are a success – do you know why and do you know how to build on it?

When did you last make a mistake? Did you tell anyone?

When did you last change your mind? Did you tell anyone why?

8.4   Check the tone of Your organization

8.4.1   The objective: to ensure that the tone you are setting sustains the organization and supports the delivery of its objectives

You set the tone – how would you define it – as of now?

Define the tone that you want and develop a plan for closing the gaps.

Describe your reputation and the behaviors that built it – is this in alignment with the tone that you want to set?

When did you last check or stop to think what effect you are having on the style and performance of those around you?

Who gives you honest and objective feedback on your performance as a leader of your organization (i.e. regardless of whether or not the organization is "delivering the numbers")?

How would each of your stakeholders describe you and your organization?

Articulate the kinds of behaviors that you believe will deliver the tone that you wish to set. What will people be doing? What will people be saying?

Why will such behaviors make you successful?

Describe the impact and effect of the tone that you want to set.

How will you ensure that your behavior and the tone that you set deliver the necessary optimum organizational performance?

Who will hurt if you fail? Who will hurt if you succeed? What will you do about it?

We all have prejudices, do you know what yours are?

What impact do your prejudices have on your performance?

8.5 People

8.5.1 The objective: to have the best team and get the best out of everyone

It starts with recruitment – no compromise – if in doubt don't hire.

Define the core competencies that are required by the organization and its objectives. These are the skills, behaviors, values and motives that will deliver success.

Match skills to jobs and tasks.

Ensure that your top team has a mixture of task and process skills. This means ensuring that the members of the team not only know what to do, but how to do it and how what they do needs to fit in order to contribute to the overall performance of the organization.

Listen and observe as much as you talk. Choose the language that you use, making sure that it encourages consistent and effective communication between as many people as possible.

Look and listen out for the "faint" messages and the "weak" signals.

Don't duck the difficult conversations. Prepare for them – have them – and tell it how it is. They provide you with opportunities to raise and reinforce standards.

Take the tough decisions concerning people (but take them kindly and with compassion). The whole organization will benefit.

It's OK to have and to show that you have feelings. Think about and then use the right language and let people know how you feel – this reinforces the messages you need to convey.

We tend to think of news as being either good or bad. There is only one sort of news to give people – that is honest news.

When people are in trouble or being made redundant, it is the moment to be kind. If possible be charitable and generous too. This is one way of letting the world know the kind of person you are and the kind of organization you are leading.

8.6   Make changes that work

8.6.1   The objective: to improve performance and stay in touch with context

Successful change is led from the top. There must be clarity of purpose and a compelling reason for making the changes that you intend to make. Build in optimism from the start while acknowledging that every change is going to be uncomfortable for someone.

Your planning must be comprehensive and complete, while acknowledging the need to be flexible and responsive to the unexpected.

The plan should attend to task, structure, processes and people as well as to strategy.

Find, develop and put in place the team that is most likely to deliver the changes. Ensure that your most-skilled people are driving the process. Note the paradox that those who are likely to be the most successful in bringing about the changes you wish to see are likely to be those who you can least spare from what they are already doing.

Only use external consultants in support of your goals and only for limited and specific purposes. Remember that you cannot delegate to consultants or to specialists, they can assist but responsibility remains yours and yours alone.

Prepare everyone who will be affected by the changes. Give your staff the confidence to embrace the changes and make the most of them. Build a supporting climate.

When pain is caused by the changes, acknowledge it, plan to minimize it, and then manage its consequences with kindness.

Look for the barriers and for potential sources of resistance to change and then take pre-emptive action to remove them. Change is more successful when it involves people's active participation, rather than when it is done to them.

Communicate continuously to build support and a sense of purpose and urgency.

Build into the plan some quick wins – nothing succeeds like success.

Look out for the paradoxes and meet them head on with "Yes and" not with "Yes but."

Look for and articulate the changes in context as they (the changes) unfold – then determine what their implications are and what your responses will be.

Reward success and focus on correcting mistakes rather than on fault-finding. Blame is not the name of the game – it results in errors being hidden or denied.

8.7   Articulate the changing context

8.7.1   The objective: to ensure that the actions of your organization are compatible with changing circumstances and stakeholder expectations, thus improving performance

There are four inevitabilities – death, taxes, change and the unexpected – you cannot evade them but you can and must take action to manage them all appropriately.

Everything around you is changing. Monitor the changes closely and determine the implications for you and your organization. Investigate how to react in order to optimize your effectiveness.

Look out for the unintended consequences of planned action.

Where is your personal focus primarily directed?

>   Inward?

>   Outward?

Where is your dominant contextual-perspective?

>   Internal?

>   External?

Where are you vulnerable?

Regularly revisit your business model and determine how it is being affected by internal and external changes.

In addition to annual accounts, establish the trends of your key performance indicators over a period of years – what do the numbers and the graphs tell you?

8.8 Speed is a core competence

8.8.1 The objective: to gain and keep the advantage

Develop a clear, well-understood and well-communicated business or operating plan, ensuring that it is widely shared and flexible enough to absorb the unexpected.

Organize to maximize knowledge about your business and all that surrounds it throughout your organization. Remember: Keep it simple but never oversimplify.

Have clear definitions of authority. Be vigilant for the gray areas and try to understand why they are there, for these are the areas where confusion and error are likely to occur.

Keep decision-making and communication-paths short.

Maintain close links with those areas in which opportunities may arise.

Share information widely within the organization to take advantage of possible synergies.

Review regularly and frequently changes in substance or context (both internal and external).

Ensure that bad news travels fast so that time is available to take mitigating action.

When things go wrong take ownership immediately. Be open and honest and focus on remedial action but never forget to stay in touch with context.

8.9 Articulate your values and your touchstones

8.9.1 The objective: to put in place the behaviors that will define and guide your organization's progress

Determining your own and your organization's touchstones gives you a set of fixed points of reference against which you can check and evaluate actions and policy under any set of circumstances – especially when the unexpected happens, as it always will.

I will always …

I will never …

Therefore:

We will always…

We will never …

On the first full day of his presidency, president Barack Obama announced that the touchstones of his administration would be transparency and the rule of law.

This statement is clear and simple and has profound implications.

Chapter 1   Introductions and a problem

1. The British psychologist Oliver James has been an increasingly vociferous critic of the way that British society has been developing in the twenty-first century. Affluenza, written a year or so before the economic crisis of 2008, makes salutary reading (Oliver James, Affluenza, Vermillion, London, 2007).

Chapter 2   The Core Issue – the unexpected is inevitable

1. Karl E. Weick is the Rensis Likert Collegiate Professor of Organizational Behavior and Professor of psychology at the University of Michigan Business School. He has written a number of seminal books on the theory of organizations. The one quoted here is Managing the unexpected (Karl E. Weick and Kathleen M. Sutcliffe, Jossey-Bass, San Francisco, 2001).
Two books that were written during the course of the recessions and fashionable use of euphemisms such as "downsizing" and "rightsizing" for the act of making people redundant are highly relevant today. These two books are:
2. David K. Hurst, Crisis and renewal: meeting the challenge of organizational change, Harvard Business School Press, Boston, 1995 and
3. David M. Noer, Healing the wounds: overcoming the trauma of layoffs and revitalizing downsized organizations, Jossey-Bass, San Francisco, 1993.
4. Chris Argyris has been a prolific author for many years. Graham has been particularly influenced by two seminal books written by Professor Argyris over 30 years ago: Chris Argyris, Increasing leadership effectiveness, John Wiley & Sons, New York, 1976 and Chris Argyris and Donald A. Schön, Theory in practice: increasing professional effectiveness, Jossey-Bass, San Francisco, 1974.
5. Karl E. Weick and Kathleen Sutcliffe (ibid.)
6. Jim Collins has written two particularly positive and sane books about the characteristics of organizations that have been consistently successful over extended periods of time. The one that we have quoted here is Good to great, Jim Collins, Random House, London, 2001. The other is Built to last: successful habits of visionary companies, James C., Collins and Jerry I. Porras, Random House, London, 1994.

7. 'Hubris Syndrome: An acquired personality disorder? A study of US Presidents and UK Prime Ministers over the last 100 years', David Owen and Jonathan Davidson, Brain, Oxford University Press, 2009.

Chapter 3   Attitudes and the unexpected

1. Socrates: "The unexamined life is a life not worth living."
2. The idea of the "undermind" is taken from Guy Claxton's delightful little book: "Hare brain, tortoise mind: why intelligence increases when you think less", Fourth Estate, London, 1998.
3. Karl E. Weick and Kathleen M. Sutcliffe, Managing the unexpected, Jossey Bass, San Francisco, 2001.
4. We have used the Margerison-McCann Team Management Resource and the Myers Briggs Type Index over many years and found them both to be very useful in helping to increase self-awareness among groups of directors and senior managers. Others swear by Belbin Team Roles for the same purpose.
5. Weick and Sutcliffe (ibid.)
6. Jean Piaget
7. Paul Z. Jackson and Mark McKergow, The solutions focus: the simple way to positive change, Nicholas Brealey, 2002.
8. Weick and Sutcliffe (ibid.)

Chapter 4   No surprises – anticipating and preparing for the unexpected

1. Karl E. Weick and Kathleen Sutcliffe, Managing the unexpected, Jossey Bass, San Francisco, 2001.
2. Jan Carlzon, Moments of truth, Harper Perennial, New York, 1987.
3. Tom Peters and Robert Waterman, In search of excellence, Harper and Row, New York, 1982.
4. Charles Handy, The Hungry Spirit, Hutchinson Arrow Books, London, 1997.
5. Karl E. Weick and Kathleen M. Sutcliffe, Managing the unexpected, Jossey-Bass, San Francisco, 2002, page 92.
6. Weick and Sutcliffe, (ibid.), page 92.
7. Jim Collins, Good to Great, Random House Business Books, London, 2001.
8. Arie de Geus, The Living Company, Nicholas Brealy, London, 1997.
9. Arie de Geus, (ibid.), page 62.
10. Yiannis Gabriel, Storytelling in organizations: facts, fictions and fantasies, Oxford University Press, Oxford, 2000, page 18.

Chapter 5   Understanding context – inside the organization

1. Peter Honey, Explore Your Values, Peter Honey Publications Limited, Maidenhead, 1999.
2. Jim Collins, Good to Great, Random House, London, 2001.

Chapter 6   Marshalling resources – building and managing commitment

1. W. J. Reddin, Managerial Effectiveness, McGraw Hill, New York, 1970.
2. E. F. L. Brech, Longmans, The Principles and Practice of Management, London, 1963; Stafford Beer, Decision and Control, John Wiley, London, 1966; and E. J. Miller and A. K. Rice, Systems of organization, Tavistock Publications, London, 1967.
3. John Darwin, Philip Johnson and J. McCauley, Developing strategies for change, Pearson, London, 2002.
4. Darwin, Johnson and McCauley, (ibid.)
5. Jim Collins, Good to Great, Random House Business Books, London 2001.

Chapter 7   Context is key – outside the organization

1. Oliver James, Affluenza, Vermillion, London, 2007; and Oliver James, The Selfish Capitalist, Vermillion, London, 2008.
2. Madeleine Bunting, Willing slaves: how the overwork culture is ruling our lives, Harper Collins, London, 2004.

actions convey messages, 33
acts of faith, 114–117
Affluenza, 12, 156
airline pilot, 35–6
aligning resources, 92
Allied Irish Bank, 26
Amoco Cadiz, 112
Anderson, Lindsay, 108
Apple, 8
Applegarth, Adam, 1
Apprentice, The, 12
Argyris, Chris   30–3, 37, 43
Assessment Centres, 54–5
assumptions, 64–7
attitudes and leadership,
     75–7
auto manufacturers, US, 69

balanced scorecard, 128
Beeching, Dr, 95
bottom line, 16
boundaries, 35
Branson, Richard, 10, 53
brewing market, 135
Browne, Lord, 53
Bunting, Madeleine, 168
business
     boutique, 156
     planning, 60
     process re-engineering,
          128
     redefining your, 135–9
     'speak', 60

call centres, 39–40
Carlzon, Jan, 80–1
categorisation, 60

change projects, 60
     saboteurs of, 140–2
     successful, 170–4, 184–6
Civil Service, 8
climate, organisational, 17
cognitive behavioural therapy,
     110
Cohen, Nick, 2
colleagues, 134
Collins, Jim, 45, 93, 115, 142
comfort zones, 136
commitment, 15, 105, 146
communication, 13, 146
communities of practice, 125
competitors and suppliers,
     159–60
competitors, 134
computer graphics, 169
consciousness, 54
consistent messages, 68–70
consultants, external, 173
Context, 3,15,16,45,105,175
     external, 150–63
     internal, 163–9
     managing changes in, 186
contextual perspective, 61,
     151–3
Cook, Peter, 79
core competence, 128
Corneille, Pierre, 52
corporate culture, 65
credit crunch, 12
     past, 155–8
crisis, 85–6
customer service, 40
customers, 134
cycle, economic, 26

Dalai Lama, 10
Davidson, Jonathan, 45
de Geus, Arie, 96, 98
difficult conversations, 44, 142
disaster recovery, 15
downshift, 11–13, 156

Einstein, Albert, 10
employees, 134
engagement, 122
Enron, 12
error
    avoidable, 14
    existence of, 30–3
ethics, 9
expectations, 55
    challenging, 57–60
experts, 72–4

finance sector, calls for
    regulation, 5
Frisch, Max, 108
Fuld, Richard, 1, 9, 111
future, shaping the, 16

Gabriel, Yiannis, 99
gaming technology, 169
Gates, Bill, 53
Goldman Sachs, 8

Handy, Charles, 84–5
Hare, David, 66
Henry V, 10
Herzberg, Frederick, 11
Honey, Peter, 109
hubris, 26, 176
    symptoms of, 45–9
Hurst, David K., 29

imaginative-emotional
    thinking, 129–31
information overload, 6,
    168
integrated thinking, 134

integrity, 16, 39
    personal, 79
internet, broadband, 118
intuition, 20

Jackson, Paul, 74
James, Oliver, 12, 156
Jobs, Steve, 53
John Lewis Partnership, 8

Katrina, hurricane, 25
Kimberley Clark, 162
knowledge
    saturation, 6
    tacit, 20, 54

language, 7, 13, 60–1, 97, 133,
    147–9, 167
    formal, 123–8
    informal, 129–31
leadership, 147–8
    a moral activity, 9
    choice and challenge, 7–10
    choices, 10–3
    integrative role of, 160
    obligations, 104–5
    organisational, style, 9
    style, 41–2
leading your organisation, 49–50
league tables, 16
Lehman Brothers, 1, 9, 26
luck, 63

Macmillan, Harold, 79
management
    by example, 42
    by exception, 83–4
    consultants, 72–4
Marks and Spencer, 8
Maxwell, Robert, 53
McKergow, Mark, 74
memories of the future, 79, 96
mentor, 46, 48
Metal Box, 162

mindlessness, 93
mindset, 41–3, 89
mirror, looking in, 181–2
morale, 138
myths, 67–8

NASA, 41
networks, 167–8
Noer, David M., 29
Northern Rock, 1, 26, 59

Obama, Barrack, 133, 188
obligations, 15
oil price rise, 28
organisation charts, 164–6
organisations, high reliability, 35
Owen, Lord David, 45

paradox, 3, 42, 117–20,
    175
people decisions, 143
personal focus, 61, 151
Peters, Tom, 81
Piaget, Jean, 72
Pinter, Harold, 66
policies and procedures, 44, 86–93
political extremism, 155
preparation, 14
procedure, 7
process, 7, 163
professional, 106–7
professional behaviour, 106–7
project management, 60
psychology, cognitive, 64

quantum physics, 118
questionnaires, psychometric, 57

recession, 13, 153–4
Reddin, Bill, 124
reflection, 20, 48, 53, 58, 161
    making time for, 44, 176, 180–1
religious fundamentalism, 155
remuneration, 11

risk management, 15
rules and procedures, 35
Rumsfeld, Donald, 19

saboteurs, 140–2
SAP, 128
Scenario Planning, 96–8
self-awareness, 9–10
self-insight, 10, 14, 48
selfish capitalism, 156
Shakespeare, William, 66
shareholder value, 145
shareholders, 134
Shell International, 96
signals, 41–3
    external, 160–1
    weak, 79, 160
six sigma, 128
Smith, Brian, 162
Smith, Darwin, 162
snakepits, 131
speed, as a competence, 187
stakeholders, 105, 134, 144
Starbucks, 8
Stoppard, Tom, 66
stories, 65, 67–8
story telling, 94
structure, and standards, 7
Sugar, Sir Alan, 53
supermarkets, 156
suppliers, 134
survivor syndrome, 156
Sutcliffe, Kathleen, 23, 35, 56, 75,
    78, 92–3
SWOT analysis, 131

takeover bid, 62
targets, 16, 66
team building, 183–4
theories
    espoused, 36
    in-use, 36
thinking
    "left brain", 122

"right brain", 122
rational-analytic, 123–9
    integrated, 147
tone, 104
    checking the, 182–3
    organisational, 15
    setting, 51–3
toolkits, 131
touchstones, 3, 79–82, 85, 108–14,
    175, 187–8
toxic debt, 153
trust, 147–8
tsunami, boxing day 2004, 25

undermind, the, 54
unexpected events
    anticipating, 15
    being unprepared for, 13–5
    effective preparation, 174–8
    genuine, 24, 49
    inevitability of, 2

of cumulative consequence, 24, 30, 49
    preparing for, 3, 99–101
    preplanning for, 101–3
    two sources of, 23–7
unreasonable truths, 117

values, 37–8, 107–14
    culture and, 7
    leading to action, 115–7
    organisational, 39
    personal, 3
    shared, 9
Virgin, 8
vision, 9, 105

Weick, Karl, 23, 35, 56, 75,
    78, 92–3
Welch, Jack, 53
white water rafting, 23
work-life balance, 11